B E N T

MART

LIBRARY - F.K.C.C.

LIBRARY
FLORIDA KEYS COMMUNITY COLLEGE
Stock Island
Key West, Florida 33040

No part of this book may be reproduced, stored in a retrieval system,
or transmitted in any form, by any means, including mechanical,
electronic, photocopying, recording, or otherwise, without the prior
written permission of the publisher.

SAMUEL FRENCH, INC.
25 WEST 45TH STREET   NEW YORK 10036
7623 SUNSET BOULEVARD   HOLLYWOOD 90046
LONDON   *TORONTO*

29049

Copyright ©, 1979, by Martin Sherman

ALL RIGHTS RESERVED

CAUTION: *Professionals and amateurs are hereby warned that BENT* *subject to a royalty. It is fully protected under the copyright laws of* *United States of America, the British Commonwealth, including Canada* *and all other countries of the Copyright Union. All rights, including profe* *sional, amateur, motion pictures, recitation, lecturing, public reading, rad* *broadcasting, television, and the rights of translation into foreign languag* *are strictly reserved. In its present form the play is dedicated to the readir* *public only.*

BENT may be given stage presentation by amateurs upon payment of *royalty of Fifty Dollars for the first performance, and Forty Dollars for ea* *additional performance, payable one week before the date when the play* *given to Samuel French, Inc., at 25 West 45th Street, New York, N.Y. 1003* *or at 7623 Sunset Boulevard, Hollywood, Calif. 90046, or to Samuel Fren* *(Canada), Ltd., 80 Richmond Street East, Toronto, Ontario, Canada M5* *1P1.*

Royalty of the required amount must be paid whether the play is presente *for charity or gain and whether or not admission is charged.*

Stock royalty quoted on application to Samuel French, Inc.

For all other rights than those stipulated above, apply to Fifi Oscard Age *cy, 19 West 44th Street, New York, N.Y. 10036.*

Particular emphasis is laid on the question of amateur or profession *readings, permission and terms for which must be secured in writing fro* *Samuel French, Inc.*

Copying from this book in whole or in part is strictly forbidden by law *and the right of performance is not transferable.*

Whenever the play is produced the following notice must appear on all pro *grams, printing and advertising for the play: "Produced by special arrang* *ment with Samuel French, Inc."*

Due authorship credit must be given on all programs, printing and adve *tising for the play.*

Anyone presenting the play shall not commit or authorize any act or omission by which the copyright of the play or the right to copyright same may be impaired.

No changes shall be made in the play for the purpose of your production unless authorized in writing.

The publication of this play does not imply that it is necessarily available for performance by amateurs or professionals. Amateurs and professionals considering a production are strongly advised in their own interests to apply to Samuel French, Inc., for consent before starting rehearsals, advertising, or booking a theatre or hall.

Printed in U.S.A.

ISBN 0 573 64031 9

GRETA: In his late thirties, Greta is a man dressed as a woman, in silver dress, top hat, and cane . . . he/she presents an appearance that is at once elegant and bizarre. He is the tough, practical proprietor of a gay nightclub who entertains the patrons by singing in a smoky, seductive voice. However, since the onslaught of the Nazis, "queen clubs are no longer cool" . . . so Greta's decided to go back to his wife and kids. . . (1-1-13)

UNCLE FREDDIE: He is an aristocratic, well-dressed gentleman in his early fifties. Max's uncle, he is a "closet fluff" . . . a homosexual who masks his predilections with a wife and children for the sake of his prestigious family name. He tries to convince Max to desert his lover Rudy and return to his family, to no avail. . . (1-3-21)

5 GERMAN SOLDIERS: rough, menacing, intense features, late 40's.

STORY LINE

Max and Rudy, homosexuals in Nazi Berlin, make an unfortunate choice of a pick-up partner, and invite a person on the Nazi's wanted list into their home. They are guilty by association, and also because they are homosexuals, whom the Gestapo are hunting down as ardently as the Jews. They manage to elude capture for two years, and Max beseeches his UNCLE FREDDIE to secure two tickets to Amsterdam, but Max and Rudy are captured by the Nazis. En route to Dachau, Rudy is slain, and the horrified Max is forced to assist in his lover's death. Max is befriended by the kindly "pink triangle (homosexual) HORST, who schools Max in the brutal realities of war. Max denies that he is a homosexual, preferring to wear the badge of the less hated Jews instead. He and Horst form a strong, psychic bond, and although they cannot touch one another on fear of death, they manage to become lovers through a vivid, imagination "lovemaking." They rely upon each other for companionship, affection, and simply to maintain their sanity. Eventually, Horst is exterminated, and Max, in a brave gesture, dons his friends uniform jacket . . . the one with the "pink triangle" which brands the wearer as a homosexual. . .

for

Alan Pope and Peter Whitman

6

CAST
(in order of appearance)

MAX . . . . *Richard Gere*
RUDY . . . . *David Marshall Grant*
WOLF . . . . *James Remar*
GUARD . . . . *Kai Wulff*
GUARD . . . . *Philip Kraus*
GRETA . . . . *Michael Gross*
UNCLE FREDDIE . . . . *George Hall*
OFFICER . . . . *Bryan E. Clark*
GUARD . . . . *John Snyder*
HORST . . . . *David Dukes*
CAPTAIN . . . . *Ron Randell*
DIRECTOR . . . . *Robert Allan Ackerman*
MUSIC . . . . *Stanley Silverman*

7

NEW APOLLO THEATRE

OPERATED BY MIDTOWN THEATRE CORPORATION

JACK STEVEN
SCHLISSEL STEINLAUF
present

RICHARD GERE

in

BENT

by

MARTIN SHERMAN

also starring

DAVID DUKES

with

RON RANDELL GEORGE HALL
JAMES REMAR MICHAEL GROSS

Bryan E. Clark Philip Kraus John Snyder Kai Wulff

and **DAVID MARSHALL GRANT**

Settings by	Lighting by	Costumes by
SANTO	ARDEN	ROBERT
LOQUASTO	FINGERHUT	WOJEWODSKI

Music by Stanley Silverman

Co-Produced by LEE MINSKOFF and PATTY GRUBMAN

Directed by

ROBERT ALLAN ACKERMAN

Initially presented by the National Playwrights Conference
at the Eugene O'Neill Memorial Center

8

BENT

ACT ONE

Scene One

(*The living room of an apartment. Small. Sparse furniture. A table with plants. A door on left leads to the outside hall. Nearby is an exit to the kitchen. At right, an exit to the bedroom, and nearby an exit to the bathroom.*)

(MAX *enters from bedroom wearing a bathrobe and is staggering from a hangover. He is having great difficulty dealing with the reality of being awake. He bumps into the plant stand. He works his way stage left along the upper wall. He turns off the radio, goes into the bathroom, turns on the light.*)

MAX. Oh God! (*Sees himself in the mirror*) Oh God!

(RUDY *enters from the kitchen, looks about the room. He goes to the side table SL, picks up bottle and 2 glasses. MAX gargles and spits. RUDY notices and, as he exits with glasses and bottle, he turns on radio. As RUDY exits into kitchen MAX comes out of bathroom. He turns off radio and staggers to footstool. He manages to sit on stool, winces and stands as he feels bruise on right buttocks. He falls into armchair, placing cushions beneath him. As he settles into chair, RUDY enters from kitchen with cup of coffee. He comes above side table and offers coffee. MAX does not react.*)

9

RUDY. Here. (*Hands* MAX *the cup;* MAX *stares and doesn't take it*) Here. (RUDY *passes coffee under* MAX'S *nose*) Coffee!

MAX. (MAX *takes coffee*) Thanks.

(RUDY *leans over and kisses* MAX. MAX *sips at coffee.* RUDY *surveys the apartment, slaps his hands together. He is deliberately irritating* MAX, *successfully.*)

RUDY. It's late. It's almost three. We really slept. (RUDY *crosses his arms. Looks about. His chatter is constant*) I missed class. (RUDY *crosses to lower L corner of chaise, picks up glass*) I hate to dance when I miss class. Bad for the muscles. And there's no place to warm up at the club. (RUDY *crosses to above side table L with glass. He empties the ash tray into the glass — loudly.* MAX *reacts*) I hate that nightclub anyhow. The floor's no good. It's cement. You shouldn't dance on cement. It kills my ankle. They've covered it with wood. Last night, before the show, I pounded on the wood — real hard (RUDY *stomps his foot three times.* MAX *shudders at each stomp*) — and I could hear the cement. I'm going to complain. I really am. (RUDY *tosses metal ash tray on side table.* MAX *reacts.* RUDY *turns to radio, picks up glass on radio, turns on radio and exits into kitchen*)

(MAX *sits in silence and stares.*)

MAX. Oh God.

(MAX *reaches for radio. Cannot reach knob.* RUDY *returns from kitchen with watering pitcher. He moves DS, smiles at* MAX, *who returns his smile weakly.* RUDY *crosses to plants. Sees plants and screams.* MAX *startled.*)

RUDY. The plants are dying. (RUDY *shows* MAX *a plant from DS of stand*) The light's bad in this apartment. (RUDY *returns the plant to the stand and waters each plant on top shelf as he chatters*) I wish we had a decent place. I wish one of your deals would come through again. Oh, listen to me, wanting a bigger place. (RUDY *kneels and waters plants on lower shelf*) Rosen's gonna be knocking on our door any minute now, you know that, wanting his rent. We're three weeks over-due. He always comes on a Sunday. What's three weeks? He can wait. Well, at least I got the new job. (RUDY *crosses to radio and waters plants on radio*) I'll get paid Thursday. If Greta keeps the club open. Business stinks. Well, I guess it means I can't complain about the cement, huh? The thing is, I don't want to dance with a bad ankle. (RUDY *crosses to kitchen door. He turns to* MAX) More coffee?

(MAX *holds out cup.* RUDY *gets cup and exits into kitchen.* MAX *takes his feet off footstool, tosses pillows DSL, leans back, closes eyes, takes a deep breath.*)

MAX. One. Two. Three. Four. Five. (MAX *takes second deep breath. Feet on footstool*) Six. Seven. Eight. Nine. Ten.

(RUDY *returns from kitchen, gives* MAX *cup of coffee.* RUDY *crosses DSR whistling. He waters plants DR.*)

MAX. O.K. Tell me.
RUDY. What?
MAX. You know.
RUDY. No.
MAX. Come on.
RUDY. I *don't* know. (RUDY *sits right side of chaise*) Listen, do you think I should ask Lena for the rent money? She's such a good person. No feeling for music though. Which is crazy, she's got such a good line. (RUDY *exends right leg in full extension*) Perfect legs.

(RUDY *crosses to footstool on next lines*) Teddy wants to do a dance for her in total silence. You think that's a good idea? (RUDY *sits on DS side footstool, pushing* MAX'S *feet off stool*) There's no place to do it though. There's no work. Lena lost that touring job. So she must be broke. So she can't lend us the money. (RUDY *stands and starts US to kitchen.* MAX *grabs his right arm.* RUDY *leaves watering pitcher at right of footstool*) Want some food?

MAX. Just tell me.

      (*Through next lines they have a tug of war*)

RUDY. What?

MAX. Must really be bad.

RUDY. What must?

MAX. That's why you won't tell me.

RUDY. Tell you what?

MAX. Don't play games.

RUDY. I'm not playing anything.

MAX. I'll hate myself, won't I? (*Silence*) Won't I?

RUDY. I'll make some breakfast. (RUDY *crosses to kitchen door. Turns to* MAX.)

MAX. Was I really rotten?

RUDY. Eggs and cheese. (RUDY *exits into kitchen*)

MAX. I don't want eggs.

RUDY. Well, we're lucky to have them. I stole them from the club. They don't need eggs. (RUDY *enters from kitchen and crosses UC*) People go there to drink. And see a terriffic show. Oh boy that's funny, cause that show stinks. You know, I'm so embarrassed, I have to think of other things while I'm dancing. (RUDY *crosses to chaise and picks up clothes, hangs shirts on front door hooks. Moves L of C folding trousers*) I have to think of grocery lists, they can tell, out there, that you're not thinking about straw hats or water lilies —

MAX. Stop!

RUDY. I mean, it really shows; particularly when it's grocery lists. Your face looks real depressed, when you can't afford groceries . . .

(MAX *moves behind* RUDY. *He embraces* RUDY, *hand over* RUDY'S *mouth.* MAX'S *head right of* RUDY'S.)

MAX. Stop it.

(RUDY *tries to speak.* MAX *tightens hand on mouth.*)

MAX. Stop it! I want to know what I did.

(MAX *releases his hand from* RUDY'S *mouth.* RUDY *kisses* MAX.)

RUDY. (*Smiles*) I love you.

(RUDY *exits into kitchen with trousers.* MAX *pauses for a moment then, on next line, he crosses to planter stand, takes one plant in each hand and crosses UC.*)

MAX. Rudy! Your plants! I'll pull the little bastards out by the roots unless you tell me.

(RUDY *enters from kitchen, crosses DS, below and right of* MAX *as* MAX *holds plants behind him and counters left. Through next lines* RUDY *attempts to get plants by reaching behind* MAX. *They circle once.*)

RUDY. No you won't.
MAX. Like to bet. I did last week.
RUDY. You killed one. That was mean.
MAX. I'll do it again.
RUDY. Don't touch them. (RUDY *grabs plants, turns and faces DR, talking to the plants*) You have to be nice to plants. They can hear you and everything. (*To the plants*) He's sorry. He didn't mean it. He's just hung over.

MAX. (MAX *leans into* RUDY'S *left*) What did I do?

(*Silence.*)

RUDY. (RUDY *returns plants to stand. Through next speech he crosses above* MAX *to left side table, picks up cup.*) Nothing much.

MAX. I can't remember a thing. And when I can't remember, it means . . .

RUDY. It doesn't mean anything. You drank a lot. That's all. The usual.

(*From CS* MAX *faces* RUDY *and lowers left shoulder of his robe to expose a bruise.*)

MAX. How'd I get this?

RUDY. (RUDY *puts down cup and crosses to* MAX. *He examines the bruise*) What's that?

MAX. Ouch! (MAX *pulls away*) Don't touch it.

RUDY. I want to see it.

MAX. So *look*. You don't have to touch.

RUDY. What is it?

MAX. What does it look like? A big black and blue mark. (MAX *turns around to* RUDY. *He pulls up robe and shows* RUDY *bruise on his left buttocks.*) There's another one here. (*Shows a mark on his arm*)

RUDY. Oh.

MAX. How did I get them?

RUDY. You fell. (RUDY *removes and cleans his glasses with his robe.*)

MAX. How?

RUDY. Someone pushed you.

MAX. Who?

RUDY. Some guy.

MAX. What guy?

RUDY. Nicky's friend.

MAX. Who's Nicky?

RUDY. One of the waiters at the club.

MAX. Which one?

RUDY. The red head.

MAX. (MAX *crosses to the chaise*) I don't remember him.

RUDY. He's a little fat.

MAX. (MAX *reclines on the chaise — on his left side, protecting his right buttocks*) Why'd the guy push me?

RUDY. (RUDY *crosses to left of chaise*) You asked Nicky to come home with us.

MAX. I did?

RUDY. Yeah.

MAX. But he's *fat*.

RUDY. Only a little.

MAX. A threesome with a fat person?

RUDY. Not a threesome. A twelvesome. You asked *all* the waiters. All at the same time too. You were standing on a table, making a general offer.

(RUDY & MAX *laugh at this.* MAX *is enjoying this story. He lies back, still protecting his buttock.*)

MAX. Oh. Then what?

RUDY. Nicky's friend pushed you off the table.

MAX. And . . .

RUDY. You landed on the floor, on top of some guy in leather.

MAX. What was he doing on the floor?

RUDY. I don't know. (RUDY *picks up paper from floor and folds it*)

MAX. Was Greta mad?

RUDY. Greta wasn't *happy*. (*Pause*) It was late. Most everyone was gone. And you were very drunk. People like you drunk. (RUDY *pats* MAX *on head with newspaper, crosses to left side table, gets cup.*) (*Pause*) I'll make some food. (RUDY *goes to the kitchen door*)

MAX. I don't want food. Why didn't you stop me?

RUDY. (RUDY *stops and turns to* MAX) How can I stop you.

MAX. Don't let me drink.

RUDY. Oh. Sure. When you're depressed?

MAX. Was I depressed?

RUDY. Of course.

MAX. I don't remember why.

RUDY. Then drinking worked, didn't it?

(RUDY *exits into kitchen. Pause.* WOLF *enters from bedroom, crosses to USL of chaise. He faces* MAX, *stretches and smiles. He is naked.* MAX *stares at him.*)

BLOND MAN. Good morning.

(WOLF *goes into bathroom.* MAX *sits up and stares at bedroom. Pause.*)

MAX. Rudy!

RUDY. (RUDY *enters from kitchen, carries dish cloth, stops just inside door*) What?

MAX. Who was that?

RUDY. Who was what?

MAX. (MAX *stands and crosses, pointing to bathroom*) *That!* That person!

RUDY. Oh. Yeah. Him. Blond?

MAX. Yes.

RUDY. And big?

MAX. Yes.

RUDY. That's the one you fell on.

MAX. The guy in leather?

RUDY. Yes. You brought him home. (*Goes into kitchen*)

MAX. Rudy! Your plants!

RUDY. (RUDY *enters from kitchen & moves several steps DS*) You brought him home, that's all. He got you going. All that leather, all those chains. You called him your own little stormtrooper. You insulted all his friends. I don't know why they didn't beat you up, but they didn't. They left. And you brought him home.

MAX. And we had a threesome? (MAX *leans against door, hides himself in clothes*)

RUDY. (RUDY *crosses left of door*) Maybe the two of you had a threesome. Max, there is no such thing. You pick guys up. You think you're doing it for me too. You're not. I don't like it. You and the other guys always end up ignoring me anyhow. Besides, last night, you and your own little stormtrooper began to get rough with each other, and I know pain is very chic just now, but I don't like it, cause pain hurts, so I went to sleep. (RUDY *crosses to left side table, picks up cup and pours coffee in plant on side table*) Here, Walter, have some coffee.

MAX. Walter?

RUDY. I'm naming the plants. They're my friends.

(RUDY *exits with cup into kitchen.* WOLF *enters from bathroom, wrapped in a towel. He has a towel around his neck. He stops left of kitchen door. He smiles at* MAX. MAX *covers his head with shirt from hook.*)

MAX. Rudy!

(RUDY *enters from kitchen with watering pitcher. He stops short at door when he sees* WOLF.)

RUDY. Oh. There's a bathrobe in there — in the bedroom.

(RUDY *points to bedroom.* WOLF *pats* RUDY'S *right cheek. He crosses below & right of* MAX, *turns, smiles, flips at* MAX'S *buttock with neck towel, laughs and exits into bedroom. There is a moment's silence then* RUDY *crosses to footstool and sits.* MAX *lets shirt fall.*)

MAX. I'm sorry.
RUDY. It's O.K.

(MAX *drops to his knees and crawls to* RUDY *on line. He puts his head on* RUDY'S *right shoulder.*)

MAX. I'm a rotten person. Why am I so rotten? Why do I do these things? He's gorgeous though, isn't he?
(RUDY *caresses* MAX'S *head.*)
I don't remember anything. I don't remember what we did in bed. Why don't I ever remember? (MAX *sits in armchair*)
RUDY. (RUDY *embraces watering pitcher*) You were drunk. And high on coke.
MAX. That too?
RUDY. Yeah.
MAX. Whose coke?
RUDY. Anna's.
MAX. I don't remember.
RUDY. You made arrangements to pick up a shipment to sell.
MAX. A *shipment?*
RUDY. Yeah.
MAX. Christ! When?
RUDY. I don't know.
MAX. That can be a lot of rent money.
RUDY. Anna will remember.
MAX. Right. (MAX *taps* RUDY *on the arm*) Hey — rent money. (MAX *indicates* WOLF *in the bedroom*) Do you think . . . maybe . . . we could . . .
RUDY. What?
MAX. (MAX *crosses UC*) Ask.
RUDY. Who?
MAX. *Him.*
RUDY. You're kidding.
MAX. Why not?
RUDY. We don't know him.

MAX. I slept with him. I think. I wonder what it was like.

RUDY. You picked him up, one night, and you're going to ask him to loan you the rent money?

MAX. Well, you know how I am.

RUDY. Yeah.

MAX. I can talk people into things.

RUDY. *Yeah.*

MAX. I can try.

RUDY. It won't work. He thinks your're rich.

MAX. Rich?

RUDY. You told him you were rich.

MAX. Terriffic.

RUDY. And Polish.

MAX. *Polish?*

RUDY. You had an accent.

(RUDY *laughs, sets pitcher right of footstool and exits into kitchen.* WOLF *enters from bedroom and crosses DR of* MAX. *Pause.* MAX *look at him.*)

MAX. Hi.

MAN. Hi. The robe is short. I look silly.

MAX. You look o.k.

MAN. Yes? You too. (WOLF *crosses to* MAX, *holds him by the buttock and starts to nibble his chest, goes to bite left nipple.* MAX *fights him off*) Ummm . . .

MAX. Not now.

(WOLF *backs off.* MAX *straightens robe and crosses to chaise. He reclines on chaise, protecting right buttock.*)

MAN. Later then.

MAX. Yes. Later.

MAN. In the country.

MAX. The country?

MAN. Your voice is different.

MAX. Oh?

MAN. You don't have an accent.

MAX. Only when I'm drunk.

MAN. Oh.

MAX. Last night — was it good?

MAN. (WOLF *crosses to left of chaise*) What do you think?

MAX. I'm asking.

MAN. Do you have to ask?

(WOLF *stares at* MAX. RUDY *enters from kitchen with cup of coffee. He crosses UC, holds out coffee in right hand.*)

RUDY. Some coffee?

MAN. Yes. Thank you.

(WOLF *does not break stare. He holds out left hand to* RUDY. RUDY *does not move. Pause.* WOLF *turns to* RUDY, *who shifts cup from right to left hand and holds it left.* WOLF *smiles, gets coffee and crosses to sit on armchair. He sips coffee then . . .*)

This place . . .

MAX. Yes?

MAN. It's really . . . (*Stops — silence*)

MAX. Small?

MAN. Yes. Exactly.

MAX. I guess it is.

MAN. You people are strange, keeping places like this in town. I don't meet people like you too much. But you interest me, your kind.

MAX. Listen . . .

MAN. Oh look, it doesn't matter, who you are, who I am. I'm on vacation. *That* matters. The country will be nice.

(WOLF *rises and crosses to chaise with cup. He places cup on right side table, kneels US by* MAX, *pulls* MAX *up against him and massages* MAX'S *neck.* RUDY *crosses to footstool and sits DS edge.*)

MAX. What's the country?
MAN. The house. Your house. Your country house.

(MAX *looks at* RUDY *through next 9 lines.*)

MAX. My country house?
RUDY. Oh. That. I forgot to tell you about that. We're driving there this afternoon.
MAX. To our country house?
RUDY. *Your* country house.
MAX. How do we get there?
RUDY. Car.
MAX. Mine?
RUDY. Right.
MAX. Right. Why don't we stay here?

(MAX *attempts to sit up.* WOLF *pulls* MAX *back against him by shoulders.*)

MAN. Don't make jokes. You promised me two days in the country.
MAX. Your name.
MAN. Yes?
MAX. I forgot your name.
MAN. Wolf.
MAX. Wolf? (*Looking at* RUDY, MAX *laughs*) Good name.
WOLF. I didn't forget yours.

(WOLF *pulls* MAX *up by supporting under arms.*)

MAX. Down, down, Wolf.
(WOLF *releases* MAX *who then slides down and leans against* WOLF'S *thighs.*)
Look, Wolfie, I don't have a car.

WOLF. Sure you do.
MAX. No.
WOLF. You showed me. On the street. Pointed it out.
MAX. Did I? It wasn't mine.
WOLF. Not yours?
MAX. No. I don't have a house in the country either.
WOLF. Of course you do. You told me all about it.
MAX. I was joking.

WOLF. (WOLF *pushes* MAX *upright and kneels up.*) I don't like jokes. You don't want me with you, is that it? Maybe I'm not good enough for you. Not rich enough. My father made watches. That's not so wonderful. (WOLF *rises and stands left of chaise*) Is it, Baron? (*Pause*)

(MAX *looks at* RUDY. *They both laugh.*)

MAX. Baron?
RUDY. Don't look at me. *That* one I didn't know about. (RUDY *swivels US holding face*)
MAX. Baron.

(MAX *starts laughing as he lies back. There is a knock on the door*)

RUDY. (RUDY *rises and crosses to chaise, gets paper, folds it*) Rosen!
MAX. Shit!

(RUDY *crosses to left side table, gets ashtray.*)

WOLF. You like to laugh at me, Baron?

(MAX *crosses to door and checks lock.* RUDY *exits into kitchen with newspaper and ashtray. Another knock.*)

(MAX *crosses to left of* WOLF. WOLF *is facing* MAX.)

MAX. Listen, Wolf, darling, you're really very sweet
and very pretty and I like you a lot, (RUDY *enters from
kitchen and crosses ¾ to footstool*) but you see, I'm not
too terriffic, because I have a habit of getting drunk and
stoned and grand and making things up. Believe me,
I'm not a Baron. (MAX *crosses above and puts arm
around* RUDY) And this is not a Baroness. There is no
country house. There is no money. I don't have *any*
money. (MAX *crosses R of C*) Sometimes I do.
Sometimes I sell cocaine, sometimes I find people to in-
vest in business deals, sometimes . . . well, I scrounge,
see, and I'm good at it, and in a few weeks, I will have
some money again. But right now, nothing. (MAX
crosses to above RUDY, *embraces* RUDY) Rudy and I
can't pay our rent. This rent. Right here. This lousy
apartment. That's all we have. And that man knocking
at our door is our landlord. And he's going to throw us
out. Because we can't pay our rent. (MAX *crosses to left
of* WOLF) Out into the streets, Wolf, the streets (MAX
embraces WOLF) Filled with filth, vermin. (MAX *kisses*
WOLF) And lice. (MAX *kisses* WOLF) And . . . urine.
(MAX *kisses* WOLF) Urine! (MAX *kisses* WOLF) Unless
someone can help us out. Unless someone gives us a
hand. (MAX *kisses* WOLF) *That's* the truth.
(MAX *breaks the embrace and crosses to left of door.*
     WOLF *gets up and counters DS of chaise.*)
Look, you don't believe me, I'll show you. Right out
there we have, just like in the movies, the greedy
landlord. (MAX *grabs doorknob and bolt lock*) Fanfare
please.
(RUDY *makes fanfare noise while blowing on the spout
     of pitcher.*)
Here he is, the one and only, Abraham Rosen!
(MAX *slides bolt and opens door.* GUARD 1 & GUARD 2
     are standing outside (–1 SL –2 SR). MAX *sees them
     and slams door closed.*)

That's not Rosen!

(GUARDS *push door open.* MAX *stumbles back to above* RUDY. GUARDS *enter.* GUARD 1 *looks around, sees* WOLF *and points to him.*)

CAPTAIN. *HIM!*

(GUARD 2 *starts for* WOLF. WOLF *throws coffee in his face.*)

WOLF. No!

(WOLF *starts for bedroom.* GUARD'S *make for him.* WOLF *pulls plant stand between them and exits bedroom.* GUARD'S *throw plant stand out of the way and exit bedroom.* MAX *starts for door.* RUDY *stands frozen.*)

MAX. Idiot! Run!

(MAX *looks at* RUDY, *goes to him, grabs pitcher, throws it at chair, grabs* RUDY *and pulls him off front door. Beats. Gunshot.* WOLF *stumbles out bedroom, pulling curtain off the rod. He falls on chaise with head at DS end.* GUARD 1 *enters followed by* GUARD 2. GUARD 1 *goes to* WOLF, *straddles him, pulls his head up by the hair, pulls out knife.*)

CAPTAIN. Wolfgang Granz, we have an order for your arrest. You resisted. Too bad.

(GUARD 1 *leans* WOLF'S *head back and slashes his throat.* WOLF *falls back.* GUARD 1 *puts knife in sheath and exits front door, followed by* GUARD 2.)

End of Scene One

ACT ONE

Scene Two

(GRETA *sits on the trapeze. She sings in a smoky, seductive voice.*)

GRETA. Streets of Berlin
I must leave you soon
Ah!
Will you forget me?
Was I ever really here?

Find me a bar
On the cobblestoned streets
Where the boys are pretty.
I can not love
For more than one day
But one day is enough in this city.

Find me a boy
With two ocean blue eyes
And show him no pity.
Take out his eyes
He never need see
How they eat you alive in this city.

Streets of Berlin
I must leave you soon
Streets of Berlin
Do you care?
Streets of Berlin
Will you cry out
If I vanish
Into thin air?

Streets of Berlin
Will you cry out
If I vanish into air?

O.K. Victor, cut the spot. (GRETA *enters door, pulls down shade, turns on lights*) My heroes! Where are you? Schmucks!

(GRETA *crosses C on line. As* GRETA *goes to dressing table, pours coffee then adds brandy to coffee and sits at chair* MAX *crosses to door and peers out through right side of shade.* MAX *sits on chaise about RC.* GRETA *begins to freshen make-up and removes shoes.* RUDY *steps toward* GRETA.)

RUDY. Is it safe?
GRETA. What?
RUDY. For us to go home?
GRETA. You fucking queers, don't you have any brains at all? No, it's not safe.
RUDY. I want to go home.
GRETA. You can't. You can't go anyplace.

(RUDY *turns and starts for* MAX.)

RUDY. I have to get my plants.
GRETA. Oh Jesus! Forget your plants. You can't go home. You can't contact friends, so don't try to see Lena. She's a good kid, you'll get her into a lot of trouble. And you certainly can't stay here. (GRETA *stands, left leg on chair, unhooks garter, removes hose*) You understand? You have to leave Berlin.
RUDY. Why? I live here, I work here.
GRETA. No, you don't. You're fired.
RUDY. I *don't* understand. What did we do? Why should we leave? (RUDY *sits on stool*)

GRETA. Don't leave. Stay. (GRETA *crosses to L end rack, deposits run hose on shelf and gets fresh hose, returns to chair, sits and changes hose*) Be *dead* schmucks. Who gives a damn? I don't.

MAX. (MAX *looks up.*) Who was he?

GRETA. Who was who?

MAX. The blond?

GRETA. (GRETA *stops*) Wolfgang Granz. (GRETA *resumes hose routine*)

MAX. What's that mean?

GRETA. He was Karl Ernst's boyfriend.

MAX. Who's Karl Ernst?

GRETA. What kind of world do you live in? Aren't you guys ever curious about what's going on?

MAX. Greta, don't lecture. Who's Karl Ernst?

GRETA. Von Helldorf's deputy. You know Von Helldorf?

MAX. The head of the stromtroopers in Berlin.

GRETA. I don't believe it. You've actually *heard* of someone. Right. Second in command at the SA, immediately under Ernst Rohm.

RUDY. Oh. Ernst Rohm. I know him.

(GRETA & MAX *stare at* RUDY)

He's that fat queen, with those awful scars on his face, a real big shot, friend of Hitler's, runs around with a lot of beautiful boys. Goes to all the clubs; I sat at his table once. He's been *here* too, hasn't he?

MAX. Rudy, shut up.

RUDY. Why?

MAX. Just shut up, o.k.? (*To* GRETA) So?

GRETA. So Hitler had Rohm arrested last night.

MAX. You're kidding. (MAX *crosses left of* GRETA) He's Hitler's right-hand man.

GRETA. Was. He's dead. Just about anyone who's high up in the SA is dead. Your little scene on top of that table was not the big event of the evening. (GRETA *rises, crosses UC & gets dress from rack*) It was a bloody night. The city's in a panic. Didn't you see the soldiers on the streets? The SS. How'd you get here in your bathrobes? Boy, you have dumb luck, that's all. (GRETA *tosses dress on chair, gets cane and tosses it on dress*) The talk is that Rohm and his stormtroopers (MAX *sits at* GRETA'S *chair*) Von Helldorf, Ernst, your blonde friend, the lot — were planning a coup. I don't believe it. What the hell, let them kill each other, who cares? (GRETA *plays with boa and with cane*) Except, it's the end of the club. As long as Rohm was around, a queer club was still o.k. Anyhow, that's who you had, baby — Wolfgang Granz. I hope he was a good fuck. (GRETA *crosses to chair, snaps fingers indicating to* MAX *to get up.* MAX *does and crosses UL of C*) What's the difference? You picked up the wrong guy, that's all.

(GRETA *sits in chair and begins with make-up.* MAX *crosses to chaise.*)

(RUDY *crosses right of* MAX. *He puts his left hand on* MAX'S *right shoulder.*)

RUDY. We can explain to somebody. It's not like we knew him.

GRETA. Sure. Explain it all to the SS. You don't explain. Not anymore. You know, you queers are not very popular anyhow. It was just Rohm keeping you all safe. Now you're like Jews. Unloved, baby, unloved.

RUDY. How about you?

GRETA. *Me?* Everyone knows I'm not queer. I got a wife and kids. Of course that doesn't mean much these days, does it? But — I still ain't queer! As for this . . . (GRETA *does "drag" take*) I go where the money is. Was. (GRETA *picks up hand mirror, faces UC and adjusts make-up*)

MAX. (*Gets up*) Money.

GRETA. Right.

MAX. Money. (MAX *moves US of* RUDY *to left of* GRETA.) Ah! Greta!

GRETA. What's with you?

MAX. How much?

GRETA. How much what?

MAX. How much did they give you?

GRETA. (*Laughs*) Oh. (GRETA *removes flowers from vase and takes out a roll of money and holds it up to* MAX) This much.

MAX. And you told them where Granz was?

GRETA. Told them, hell—I showed them your building.

RUDY. (RUDY *crosses to sit right chaise*) Greta, you didn't.

GRETA. Why not? You don't play games with the SS. Anyhow, it's just what he would do, your big shot here. (MAX *crosses to lean on shelf of rack*) He likes money too. He just isn't very good at getting it. Me, I'm dynamite. Here. I'll do you a favor. Take it. (GRETA *peels off bills*)

RUDY. Don't take it.

GRETA. It will help.

RUDY. We don't want it.

MAX. (MAX *crosses left of* GRETA) Shut up, Rudy.

RUDY. Stop telling me to . . .

MAX. Shut up! (MAX *takes money, counts it and throws it on dressing table*) It's not enough. We want more.

GRETA. So get more.

MAX. (MAX *crosses C, turns, points to* GRETA) If they catch us, it won't help you.

GRETA. Oh? A threat? (*Pause*) Tell you what. I'll do you a favor. Take some more. (GRETA *crosses to left of door, pauses, peels a few more bills off, offers them.* MAX *holds*) I've made a lot off your kind, so I'm giving a little back. Take it all. (GRETA *offers it all*)

MAX. O.K.

(MAX *crosses to* GRETA *and takes money.* GRETA *opens door and crosses to right end of rack.*)

GRETA. Now get out.

MAX. (*To* RUDY) Come on . . .

RUDY. Where? (RUDY *turns DS*) I'm not leaving Berlin.

MAX. We have to.

RUDY. We don't have to.

MAX. They're looking for us.

RUDY. But I live here.

(MAX *shuts door.*)

MAX. Come on . . .

RUDY. I've paid up for dance class for the next two weeks.

MAX. Jesus! Come on!

RUDY. (RUDY *crosses DR of C*) If you hadn't gotten so drunk . . .

MAX. Don't.

RUDY. Why'd you have to take him home?

MAX. How do I know? *I don't remember.*

RUDY. You've ruined everything.

MAX. Right. I always do. Tell you what. Why don't we just split up right here? (MAX *crosses left of* RUDY) So you go off on your own, o.k.? Go back to dance class. They can shoot you in the middle of an arabesque. Take half. (MAX *offers* RUDY *bills*)

RUDY. I don't want it.

MAX. Then fuck it! (MAX *stuffs money in his pocket and crosses to the door*)

(GRETA *crosses to left of UC.* MAX *stops at door.*)

GRETA. Max. This one can't handle it alone. Look at him.

(GRETA *looks at* RUDY. MAX *looks at* RUDY. *Then*
    GRETA *looks at* MAX *then to* RUDY. GRETA *snaps*
    his fingers to RUDY.)
Take his hand, schmuck.
(RUDY *crosses to* MAX. *He puts his head on* MAX'S
    right shoulder. RUDY *takes* MAX'S *left hand with*
    his right hand. GRETA *counters right.*)
That's right. (GRETA *crosses to dressing table to get*
brandy)
    RUDY. Where are we going to go?
    GRETA. (GRETA *stops and turns to them*) *Don't.*
Don't say anything in front of me. Get out.

(MAX *and* RUDY *exit.* GRETA *crosses to door, closes*
    it, leans against it, takes off wig and tosses it on
    chaise. Rides wagon off.)

BLACKOUT

End of Scene Two

ACT ONE

Scene Three

Lights up on a park in Cologne.

(FRED *sets reading a newspaper on right end of bench.*
    MAX *crosses UC, crosses above left of bench, sees*
    FRED. MAX *crosses above and right of bench,*
    lights cigarette & crosses left of bench. MAX *stops*
    pacing.)

    FREDDIE. Sit down.
(MAX *sits left of bench. Both stare ahead.* FRED *folds*
    newspaper and places it on lap. They tip hats.)

Pretend we're strangers. Having a little conversation in the park. Perfectly normal. Do something innocent. (FRED *doesn't look at* MAX. *He reads*) Feed the pigeons.

MAX. There aren't any piegons.

(FRED *slides envelope to* MAX *across bench. He shifts position to look at* MAX.)

FREDDIE. Here.

(FRED *reads.* MAX *puts envelope inside his coat.*)

MAX. You look good, uncle Fredie.

FREDDIE. You look older.

MAX. What's in this?

FREDDIE. Your papers and a ticket to Amsterdam. (FRED *puts paper on lap*)

MAX. One ticket?

FREDDIE. Yes.

MAX. Shit.

(FRED *is frightened and looks around.*)

FREDDIE. Keep your voice down. Remember, we're strangers. Just a casual conversation. Perfectly normal.

MAX. One ticket. I told you on the phone . . .

FREDDIE. (*Firmly*) One ticket. That's all.

MAX. I can't take it. Damn it, I'd kill for this. Here. (MAX *slides envelope back to* FRED. *He gets up and crosses left*) Thanks anyway.

FREDDIE. (FRED *covers envelope with newspaper*) Sit down. It wasn't easy getting new papers for you. If the family finds out . . .

(MAX *sits right end bench.*)

I have to be careful. They've passed a law, you know. We're not allowed to be fluffs anymore. We're not even allowed to kiss or embrace. Or fantasize. They can arrest you for having fluff thoughts.

MAX. (MAX *laughs gently*) Oh, Uncle Freddie.

FREDDIE. It's not funny.

MAX. It is.

FREDDIE. The family takes care of me. But you. Throwing it in everyone's face. No wonder they don't want anything to do with you. Why couldn't you have been quiet about it? Settled down, gotten married, paid for a few boys on the side. No one would have known. Ach! Take this ticket. (FRED *slides newspaper and envelope across bench.*)

MAX. I can't. Stop giving it to me.

(FRED *picks up newspaper and envelope and puts it on lap.*)

FREDDIE. Look over there.

MAX. Where?

FREDDIE. Over there. (FRED *indicates off right*) See him?

MAX. Who?

FREDDIE. With the moustache.

MAX. Yes.

FREDDIE. Cute.

MAX. I guess.

FREDDIE. Think he's a fluff?

MAX. I don't care.

FREDDIE. You've been running for two years now. Haven't you? With that dancer. The family knows all about it. You can't live like that.

(FRED *puts newspaper with envelope on bench & pushes it toward* MAX. MAX *reaches down. He touches* FRED'S *hand.*)

Take this ticket.

MAX. (MAX *looks at* FRED) I need two.

FREDDIE. (FRED *looks at* MAX) I can't get two.

MAX. Of course you can.

FREDDIE. (FRED *pulls hand away and looks off right*)
Yes. I think he is a fluff. You have to be so careful now.
What is it? Do you love him?

MAX. Who?

FREDDIE. The dancer.

MAX. Jesus!

FREDDIE. Do you?

MAX. Don't be stupid. What's love? Bullshit. I'm a
grown up now. I just feel responsible.

FREDDIE. Fluffs can't afford that kind of respon-
sibility.

(MAX *laughs.*)
Why are you laughing?

MAX. That word. Fluffs. Look, do you think it's
been a holiday? (MAX *stamps out cigarette*) We've
tramped right across this country; we settle in
somewhere and then suddenly they're checking papers
and we have to leave rather quickly; now we're living
outside Cologne, in the goddman forest! In a colony of
tents — are you ready for that? *Me* in a tent! With hun-
dreds of very boring unemployed people. Except most
of them are *just* unemployed; they're not running from
the Gestapo. I'm not cut out for this, Uncle Freddie. I
was brought up to be comfortable. Like you. O.K. I've
been fooling around for too long. You're right. The
family and I should make up. So. How about a deal?
Two tickets to Amsterdam. And two new sets of identity
papers. Once we get to Amsterdam, I ditch him. And
they can have me back.

FREDDIE. Maybe they don't want you back. It's been
ten years.

MAX. They want me. It's good business. I'm an only
son. (*Pause*) Remember that marriage father wanted to
arrange? Her father had button factories too. I just read.
about her in the paper; she's an eligible widow, living in
Brussels. Make the arrangements again. I'll marry her.

Our button factories can sleep with her button factories.
It's a good deal. You know it. And eventually, when all
this blows over, you can get me back to Germany. If I
want a boy, I'll rent him. Like you. I'll be a discreet,
quiet . . . fluff. Fair enough? It's what father always
wanted. Just get us *both* out alive.

FREDDIE. I'll have to ask your father.

(MAX *turns bodily to* FRED. *Hard eye contact*.)

MAX. Do it. Then ask him.

FREDDIE. I can't do things on my own. Not now.
(FRED *indicates envelope on bench*) Just this.

MAX. I can't take it.

(FRED *picks up newspaper & envelope & puts them on
his lap. He looks off right*.)

FREDDIE. He's looking this way. He might be the
police. No. He's a fluff. He has fluff eyes.
                (MAX *turns DS*.)
Still. You can't tell. You better leave. (FRED *puts
envelope in coat*) Just be casual. Perfectly normal. I'll
ask your father.

MAX. Soon?

FREDDIE. Yes. Can I phone you? (FRED *reads*)

MAX. In the *forest?*

FREDDIE. Phone me. On Friday.

(MAX *stands & turns left of bench. He turns back to*
FRED *and faces DS*.)

MAX. You look good, Uncle Freddie.

(FRED *looks at* MAX *& tips hat. Goes back to reading*.
MAX *tips hat to* FRED. *Pauses. He exits UC. As*

MAX *exits,* FRED *drops paper. He looks off right. Small smile. He rides wagon off.)*

BLACKOUT

End of Scene Three

ACT ONE

Scene Four

The Forest.

In front of a tent.

(RUDY *enters UL, crosses to DR of C placing ruck sack right of the fire area. He crosses R of C then crosses to behind left trees, gets wood, brings it to flame area, tosses it in and lights fire. He sits. Pulls out cheese, apples and knife from pockets. They are wrapped in napkins. He smoothes napkins on lap. Blows on fire.)*

RUDY. (*Cuts first slice of cheese and leaves on point of knife. Places apples on ground*) Cheese! Max!

(MAX *enters from tent ULC carrying dufflebag. He tosses bag on ground left of fire. He stands behind it with left foot on bag.* RUDY *offers him cheese on knife.)*

(RUDY *eats cheese.* MAX *steps over bag, sits on it across from* RUDY. *He warms himself.)*

MAX. Where'd you get the cheese. Steal it?
RUDY. I don't steal. I dug a ditch.

MAX. You *what?*

RUDY. (RUDY *eats*) Dug a ditch. Right outside of Cologne. They're building a road. You can sign on each morning if you get there in time. They don't check your papers. It's good exercise too, for your shoulders. I'm getting nice shoulders. But . . . no more dancing feet. Here. (RUDY *gives* MAX *a piece of cheese.*) Eat!

MAX. I don't want food. (MAX *eats cheese*) You shouldn't have to dig ditches. I want some real food, for Christ's sake. (*Takes the cheese*) Look at this. It's lousy cheese. You don't know anything about cheese. Look at all these tents. There's no one to talk to in any of them. (MAX *eats cheese. Spits it out and holds out cheese in right hand*) It has no flavour.

RUDY. (RUDY *grabs cheese and eats it*) Then don't eat it. I'll eat it. I have apples too. (RUDY *juggles two apples*)

MAX. I hate apples.

RUDY. Then starve. (RUDY *stops juggling, then resumes*) What did you do today, while I was ditch digging?

MAX. Nothing.

RUDY. You weren't here when I got back.

MAX. Went to town.

RUDY. Have fun?

(*Quick check around.* MAX *leans in to* RUDY.)

MAX. I might get us new papers and tickets to Amsterdam.

RUDY. You said that in Hamburg.

MAX. It didn't work out in Hamburg.

RUDY. You said that in Stuttgard.

MAX. Are you going to recite the list?

RUDY. Why not? I'm tired of your deals. (RUDY *stops juggling and eats a piece of cheese*) You're right. This cheese stinks. (RUDY *puts cheese on ground*) I don't want to eat it.

(MAX *picks up cheese and gives it to* RUDY)

MAX. You have to eat.

RUDY. Throw it out. (RUDY *puts cheese on ground*)

MAX. You get sick if you don't eat.

RUDY. So what?

MAX. O.K. Get sick.

RUDY. No. I don't want to get sick. (RUDY *picks up cheese and eats it*) If I get sick, you'll leave me behind. You're just waiting for me to get sick.

MAX. Oh — here we go.

RUDY. You'd love it if I died.

MAX. (MAX *stands*) Rudy! (MAX *sits*)

RUDY. (RUDY *crosses over and sits US of* MAX *on bag.*) You know what I keep asking myself?

MAX. What?

RUDY. If we had just talked to the SS that day and explained everything — could it have been worse than this?

MAX. Maybe not.

RUDY. Maybe not. (RUDY *crosses and sits on rucksack*) You're supposed to say yes, *much* worse. Don't tell me maybe not. That's what you want. You want me to kill myself. (RUDY *peels apple*)

MAX. I just want to get us out of here. These awful tents. There's no air. We're *in* the air, but there's still no air. I can't breathe. I've got to get us across the border.

RUDY. Why don't we just cross it?

MAX. What do you mean?

RUDY. This guy, on the job today, was telling me it's easy to cross the border.

MAX. Oh, sure, it's simple. You just walk across. Of course, they shoot you.

RUDY. He said he knew spots.

MAX. Spots?

RUDY. Spots to get through. I told him to come talk to you.

MAX. *Here?*

RUDY. Yes.

MAX. (MAX *crosses US above* RUDY. *Leans in to* RUDY.) I told you we don't want anyone to know we're here, or that we're trying to cross the border. Are you *that* dumb?

RUDY. I'm not dumb.

MAX. He could tell the police.

RUDY. O.K. So I *am* dumb. Why don't we try it anyway?

MAX. Because . . .

RUDY. Why?

MAX. A deal.

RUDY. What?

MAX. (MAX *returns to sit on bag*) I'm working on a deal.

RUDY. Who with?

MAX. I can't tell you.

RUDY. Why not?

MAX. It spoils it. If I tell you about it before it happens. Then it won't happen. I'm superstitious.

RUDY. When why'd you bring it up?

MAX. So you'd know that . . .

RUDY. What?

MAX. That I'm trying.

RUDY. This is crazy. We're in the middle of the jungle . . .

MAX. Forest.

RUDY. (*Shouting*) Jungle. I'm a dancer, not Robin Hood.

(MAX *indicates to* RUDY *to lower voice.*)

I've walked my feet away. But you don't mind. You're working on deals. You worked on deals in Berlin, you work on deals in the jungle.

MAX. Forest.

RUDY. Jungle. I want to get out of here. I could have. I met a man in Frankfurt. You were in town "working on a deal." He was an old man, rich too. I could have stayed with him. I could have got him to get me out of the country. He really wanted me, I could tell. But no, I had to think about you. It wasn't fair to *you*. You're right, I'm dumb. (RUDY *throws food on ground*) You would have grabbed the chance. You're just hanging around, waiting for me to die. (RUDY *pulls coat up around ears*) I think you've poisoned the cheese.

MAX. It's *your* cheese. Choke on it. Please, choke on it. I can't tell you how much I want you to choke on it. Christ! (MAX *picks up knife, apple and cheese and puts in pocket*)

(RUDY *puts US hand on* MAX'S *US leg pulling at coat.*)

RUDY. Tell me about the deal.
MAX. No.
RUDY. Come on.
MAX. No. Absolutely not! Trust me, just trust me.
RUDY. Where are you going? (RUDY *turns away R*)

(MAX *tosses knife down on stage and crosses DR in front of trees, moving above* RUDY.)

MAX. I have to get out of here. I can't breathe. I'm going for a walk.
RUDY. (RUDY *stands*) You can't. There's no place to walk. Just tents and jungle.
MAX. I have a fever.
RUDY. What?
MAX. I have a fever! I'm burning up.
RUDY. It's a trick.

(RUDY *crosses to left of* MAX *to feel his forehead with left hand.* MAX *pulls away right.*)

MAX. I know. I'm lying. Get away.

RUDY. Let me feel. (RUDY *feels* MAX'S *forehead*) You have a fever.

MAX. It's the cheese. *You* poisoned *me*. What the hell.. (MAX *crosses and sits on US end of bag*) I'll die in the jungle.

RUDY. Forest.

(MAX & RUDY *laugh*.)

(MAX *kicks rucksack to* RUDY *indicates sit*.)

(RUDY *sits*.)

(*Silence*)

MAX. Remember cocaine?

RUDY. Yes.

MAX. I'd like cocaine.

RUDY. Yes.

MAX. What would you like?

RUDY. New glasses.

MAX. What?

RUDY. My eyes have changed. I need a new prescription. I'd like new glasses.

MAX. In Amsterdam.

RUDY. Sure.

MAX. In *Amsterdam*. Cocaine and new glasses. Trust me.

(RUDY *starts to touch* MAX *but stops himself*.)

Plants. You'll have plants. Wonderful Dutch plants. And Dutch dance classes. Your feet will come back. And you won't dig ditches. You'll have to give up your new shoulders though.

(RUDY *sits up*.)

And you know what? We can buy a Dutch dog.

(MAX & RUDY *laugh*.)

Everyone should have a dog. I don't know why we didn't have a dog in Berlin. We'll have one in Amsterdam. Trust me.

(*Pause.*)

RUDY. How's your fever?

MAX. Burning.

(RUDY *touches* MAX'S *forehead, leaving his hand on his head.*)

MAX. Don't.

RUDY. I'm sorry Max. (RUDY *strokes* MAX'S *head*)

MAX. Don't.

RUDY. I really love you.

    (RUDY *takes* MAX'S *hand on* MAX'S *US leg.*)

MAX. DON'T.

                (RUDY *pulls away*)

If they see us . . . from the other tents . . . they're always looking . . . they could throw us out . . . for touching . . . we have to be careful . . . we have to be very careful . . .

RUDY. O.K. (*Pause — starts to sing*) "Streets of Berlin"

MAX. What are you doing?

RUDY. Singing. Well, we're sitting around a campfire. That's when people sing. Just like . . . the Hitler Youth does it. They sing old favorites too. I'm sure they're not allowed to touch either.

MAX. Don't be so sure.

RUDY. Well, it's unfair if they can, and we can't. (*Sings*)

    Find me a bar

    On the cobblestone streets

BOTH:

Where the boys are pretty

(MAX *touches* RUDY'S *US leg tentatively.* RUDY *takes* MAX'S *hand.*)

Max.
I cannot love
For more than one day

(Max *takes off coat and throws it over their hands.
    They laugh.*)

BUT
One day is enough
In this city

VOICE. (*From the darkness*) There! That's them!

(Max & Rudy *stand. They cover faces with hands.
    As trains in place* Max *sits on DS end of SR unit,*
    Rudy *sits on floor next to him.*)

(*A bright light shines on* Max *and* Rudy.)

ANOTHER VOICE. (*From darkness*) Maximilian Berber.
Rudolph Hennings. Hands high in the air. You are
under arrest.

BLACKOUT

End of Scene Four

ACT ONE

Scene Five

(*A train whistle is heard.*)

(*Sound of a train running through the night. A train
    whistle again.*)

(*A circle of light comes up.*)

(*It is a prisoner transport train. We see one small corner. Five prisoners are in the light — two men in civilian dress, then* RUDY *and* MAX, *then a man, in his twenties, wearing a striped uniform, with a pink triangle sewn onto it.*)

(*A* GUARD *walks through the circle of light. He carries a rifle.*)

(*Silence.*)

(HORST *is on lower SL bunk, head DS facing off.* MAX *sits DS end of lower SR bunk.* RUDY *sits on floor at* MAX'S *left. His first line is to* MAX.)

RUDY. Where do you think they're taking us?
         (*Silence.*)
      (*The other prisoners look away.*)
   (*The* GUARD *walks through the circle of light.*)
         (*Silence.*)
     (RUDY *slides over to* HORST.)
Excuse me. (*To the* PRISONER *next to him*) Did you have a trial?
      (*The* PRISONER *doesn't answer.*)
  MAX. Rudy!
       (RUDY *returns to* MAX.)
         (*Silence.*)
(RUDY *and* MAX *look at each other. They are both terrified.* RUDY *starts to extend his hand, then withdraws it.*)
(*A scream is heard — off, beyond the circle.* RUDY *and* MAX *look at each other, then turn away.*)
         (*Silence.*)
(OFFICER *enters UC and crosses DC, left of* RUDY. GUARD 1 *follows him and stands left of him.* GUARD 2 *enters 2 beats later. He pauses half way down bunk. He rests his right foot on lower right*

bunk. RUDY *looks up at* OFFICER *then at* MAX. OF-
FICER'S *first line is to* GUARD 1 *as he notices*
RUDY'S *glasses.*)

OFFICER. Glasses. (*Silence*)
            (OFFICER *speaks to* RUDY.)
Give me your glasses.
(RUDY *hands the* OFFICER *his glasses, looking at* MAX
    then the OFFICER. OFFICER *examines glasses. He*
    shows them to GUARD 1.)
Hornrimmed. Intelligensia.
    RUDY. What?
    OFFICER. (*Smiles*) Stand up.
(RUDY *stands. He is frightened.* OFFICER *puts glasses*
    DC.)
Step on your glasses.
            (RUDY *look at* OFFICER *and* MAX.)
Step on them.
            (RUDY, *tentative, steps on glasses.*)
Take him.
(OFFICER *indicates to* GUARD 1. RUDY *grabs hold of*
    bunk. GUARD 1 & GUARD 2 *grab* RUDY *and take*
    him off UC. RUDY *fights them.*

    RUDY. Max!

(RUDY looks at MAX. *The* GUARD *pulls* RUDY *off —*
    out of the circle. The OFFICER *smiles.*)

    OFFICER. Glasses.

(OFFICER *kicks glasses toward* MAX. *He exits UC,*
    glancing at MAX.)
            (MAX *stiffens. A scream is heard.*)
                (*Silence.*)
(MAX *stands and starts around end of bunk.* RUDY
    screams again.)

(*The man wearing the pink triangle,* HORST, *moves toward* MAX. *He touches him.*)

HORST. Don't.
(*He removes his hand from* MAX *and looks straight ahead.*)
(*The* GUARD *walks through the circle of light.*)
Don't move. You can't help him.
(RUDY *screams.* MAX *turns DS.*)
(*Silence.*)

MAX. This isn't happening.
HORST. It's happening.

(MAX *notices* HORST. *He crawls to C against left bunk.*)

MAX. Where are they taking us?
HORST. Dachau.
MAX. How do you know?
HORST. I've been through transport before. They took me to Cologne for a propoganda film. Pink triangle in good health. Now it's back to Dachau.
MAX. Pink triangle? What's that?
HORST. Queer. If you're queer, that what you wear. If you're a Jew, a yellow star. Political — a red triangle. Criminal — green. Pink's the lowest. (*He looks straight ahead.*)

(*The* GUARD *walks through the circle of light.*)

(RUDY *screams.* MAX *looks off USR.*)

MAX. (MAX *covers his head with arms*) This isn't happening. This can't be happening.
HORST. Listen to me. (HORST *whispers into* MAX'S *left ear*) If you survive the train, you stand a chance. Here's where they break you. You can do nothing for your friend. Nothing —

(RUDY *screams.* MAX *hurls himself against the edge of right bunk.*)

If you try to help him, they will kill you. If you try to care for his wounds, they will kill you. (HORST *leans over edge of bunk and addresses* MAX) If you even *see*— see what they do to him, *hear* — hear what they do to him — they will kill you. If you want to stay alive, he can not exist.

(RUDY *screams.* MAX *swings himself around to end of right bunk.*)

    MAX. It isn't happening.
                   (RUDY *screams.*)
    HORST. He hasn't a chance. He wore glasses.
                   (RUDY *screams.*)
If you want to stay alive, he can not exist.
                   (RUDY *screams.*)
It *is* happening.

(HORST *lies down, turning to face left into wall. On* RUDY'S *scream* MAX *rises, is confused and sits again on end of SR bunk.*)

    MAX. It isn't happening . . . it isn't happening . . .

(GUARD 1 & GUARD 2 *drag* RUDY *on from UC. They cross DSL of C.* GUARD 1 *is left of* RUDY. GUARD 2 *is right of* RUDY. *The* OFFICER *follows to stand in front of* GUARD 2.)

    OFFICER. (OFFICER *speaks to* MAX) Who is this man?
    MAX. I don't know. (MAX *stops mumbling, looks straight ahead.*)

(OFFICER *looks at* GUARD 2, *smiles then speaks to* MAX.)

    OFFICER. Your friend?
                 (*Silence.*)

MAX. No.
                    (RUDY *moans.*)
OFFICER. Look at him.
            (MAX *does not look. He is agitated.*)
Look!
(MAX *looks at* RUDY. OFFICER *hits* RUDY *in chest while
    looking at* MAX. RUDY *screams and* MAX *looks
    away at floor.*)
Your friend?
MAX. No.

(MAX *continues to focus on floor and closes his eyes.
    The* OFFICER *hits* RUDY *in chest.* RUDY *screams.*)

OFFICER. Your friend?
MAX. No. (MAX *stares straight ahead*)
OFFICER. Hit him.
            (MAX *stares at* OFFICER *disbelieving*)
Like this.

(OFFICER *hits* RUDY *in chest.* RUDY *screams.* MAX
    stares straight ahead. He shuts his eyes.)

OFFICER. *Hit him.*
                    (MAX *doesn't move*)
Your friend?
        (OFFICER *crosses DR of* MAX, *faces* RUDY.)
Your friend?
MAX. No.

(MAX *tentatively rises. He crosses haltingly to* RUDY,
    all the while looking at OFFICER. *He closes his eyes,
    hits* RUDY *in chest and dashes back to sit DS end of
    right lower bunk. He looks at* OFFICER.)

OFFICER. Open your eyes.
                    (MAX *opens his eyes.*)
Again.

(MAX *slowly crosses to* RUDY. *He looks at* OFFICER *and, with eyes open quickly hits* RUDY *in chest.*)

Again!

      (MAX *hits* RUDY *in chest.*)

Again!

(MAX *repeatedly slugs* RUDY in chest as GUARD 1 & GUARD 2 *turn* RUDY *into* MAX.)

Enough.

(OFFICER *pulls* MAX *off.* GUARD 1 & GUARD 2 *release* RUDY, *who falls to floor below right bunk.* MAX *is at right bunk's DS end.* OFFICER *steps DSC.*)

Your friend?

    MAX. No.

    OFFICER. (*Smiles*) No.

(GUARD 1 & GUARD 2 *exit UC. There is a pause then* OFFICER *exits.* RUDY *moans and calls for* MAX. MAX *sits on DS end of right lower bunk. He closes his eyes, grabs edge of bunk and takes a deep breath.*)

    MAX. One. Two. Three. Four. Five. (MAX *takes another deep breath*) Six. Seven. Eight. Nine. Ten.

    (RUDY *calls* MAX'S *name.* MAX *stares ahead.*)

(*The lights dim on* MAX, *almost to blackout — then, suddenly, they expand, and include the three other prisoners. A morning ray of sunlight.*)

    (RUDY *lies at* MAX'S *feet.*)

(*The* GUARD *walks through the circle of light.*)

      (*Silence.*)

(*As lights come up* OFFICER *enters UC followed by* GUARD 1. OFFICER *crosses DL of C. -1 stands above him.* MAX *still at bunk. He does not acknowledge them.*)

OFFICER. Stand up.
              (MAX *rises*.)
(*Stares at* MAX) We'll see. (*To* GUARD) Take him.
(GUARD 1 *takes* MAX *and leads him off UC. The* OF-
    FICER *crosses to* RUDY, *taps him with his boot*.)
Dead.

(*The* OFFICER *exits UC. As lights go down the*
    PRISONERS *in middle bunks crawl out, pull cane
    bolts and revolve units.* HORST *crawls out of bunk.*
    KAPO *takes barrel and moves it DS of left end wall.
    All the* PRISONERS *take bowls from bunks and
    form line.* PRISONER 1 *at barrel,* PRISONER 2,
    HORST, PRISONER 3, MAX.)

End of Scene Five

ACT ONE

Scene Six

(*Lights up, on one side of the stage. A large barrel is on
    the ground. A prisoner-foreman,* KAPO, *stands
    behind the barrel, with a huge ladle. He stirs it. The*
    KAPO *wears a green triangle on his prison uniform.*
    PRISONER'S *come up, one by one, with bowls in
    their hand, to be fed. They all wear prison
    uniforms*.)

(PRISONER 1 *gets soup and crosses to left end of right
    wall & sits, facing left.* PRISONER 2 *gets soup,
    crosses to right end of left wall, faces DS.* HORST *at
    soup barrel. He gets his soup*.)

HORST. Only soup. You skimmed it from the top.

There's nothing in it but water. No meat, no vegetables .
. . Nothing.

KAPO. Take what you get.

HORST. (*Reaches for the ladle*) Give me some meat.

KAPO. (*Pushes him back*) Fucking queer! Take what
you get!

(KAPO *pushes* HORST *away*. HORST *crosses DR. As
MAX passes by* PRISONER 2 *the* PRISONER *sits.*
HORST *sits right end of right wall.* MAX *gets his
soup. He is subservient to* KAPO. MAX *crosses to
left end of right wall. He leans against wall.* KAPO
carries barrel off between walls and out UC. MAX
spots HORST *and crosses to him and sits next to
him, left of* HORST.)

(*Blackout.*)

(*Lights rise on other side of the stage.*)

(*A tight little corner at the end of the barracks.* HORST
*crawls in, and sits huddled with his bowl. He drinks
the soup.*)

(MAX *enters, crawling in next to* HORST. *He carries a
bowl. He wears the prison uniform. On it is a
yellow star.*)

MAX. Hi.

(HORST *looks at him; says nothing;* MAX *holds up his
bowl.* MAX *looks in* HORST's *bowl. He gives him
some vegetables.*)
Here.

HORST. Leave me alone.

MAX. I got extra. Some vegetables. Here. (*Drops
some vegetables from his bowl in* HORST's *bowl*)

HORST. (HORST *looks in his own bowl*) Thanks.

(*They eat quietly*)

(HORST *looks up. Stares at* MAX'S *uniform.*)

HORST. (HORST *does not look at* MAX) Yellow star?
MAX. What?
HORST. Jew?
MAX. Oh. Yeah.
HORST. I wouldn't have figured it.

(*Silence.*)

I'm sorry about your friend.
MAX. Who?
HORST. Your friend.
MAX. Oh.

(*Silence.*)

HORST. It's not very sociable in these barracks.
(*Laughs*) Is it?
MAX. (MAX *slides into* HORST *and indicates the triangle*) How'd you get the pink?
HORST. I signed a petition.
MAX. And?
HORST. That was it.
MAX. What kind of petition?
HORST. For Magnus Hirschfield.
MAX. Oh yeah. I remember him. Berlin.
HORST. Berlin.
MAX. He wanted to . . .
HORST. Make queers legal.
MAX. Right. I remember.
HORST. Looked like he would too, for a while. It was quite a movement. Then the Nazis came in. Well. I was a nurse. They said a queer couldn't be a nurse. Suppose I had to touch a patient's penis! God forbid. They said rather than be a nurse, I should be a prisoner. A more suitable occupation. So. So. That's how I got my pink triangle. How'd you get the yellow star?
MAX. I'm Jewish.
HORST. You're not Jewish, you're a queer.

(MAX *looks right & left to see who might have heard.*)

(*Silence.*)

MAX. I didn't want one.

HORST. Didn't want what?

MAX. A pink triangle. I didn't want one.

HORST. Didn't *want* one?

MAX. You told me it was the lowest. So I didn't want one.

HORST. So?

MAX. So I worked a deal.

HORST. A deal?

MAX. Sure. I'm good at that.

HORST. With the Gestapo?

MAX. Sure.

HORST. You're full of shit.

(*Silence.*)

MAX. I'm going to work a lot of deals around here. They can't keep us here forever. Sooner or later they'll release us. I'm only under protective custody, that's what they told me. I'm going to stay alive.

HORST. I don't doubt it.

MAX. Sure. I'm good at that.

HORST. Thanks for the vegetables. (HORST *starts to rise. He haunches over*)

MAX. Where are you going?

HORST. (HORST *pauses in movement*) To sleep. We get up at four in the morning. I'm on stone detail. I chop stones up. It's fun. Excuse me . . .

(HORST *starts again to rise.* MAX *stops him with his right hand.* HORST *sits back on haunches.*)

MAX. Don't go.

HORST. I'm tired.

MAX. I don't have anyone to talk to.

HORST. Talk to your lansmen.

MAX. I'm not Jewish.

HORST. Then why are you wearing that?

MAX. You told me pink was the lowest.

HORST. It is, but only because the other prisoners hate us so much.

MAX. (MAX *holds out and indicates bowl*) I got meat in my soup. You didn't.

HORST. Good for you. (HORST *rises and crosses left of* MAX.)

MAX. Don't go.

HORST. (HORST *goes into deep knee position*) Look, friendships last about twelve hours in this place. We had ours on the train. Why don't you go and bother someone else.

MAX. You didn't think I'd make it, did you? Off the train?

HORST. I wasn't sure.

MAX. I'm going to stay alive.

HORST. Yes.

MAX. Because of you. You told me how.

HORST. Yes. (*Pause*) I did. (*Pause*) I'm sorry.

MAX. About what?

HORST. I don't know. Your friend.

MAX. Oh.

(*Silence.*)

He wasn't my friend.

(*Silence.*)

HORST. You should be wearing a pink triangle.

MAX. I made a deal.

HORST. You don't make deals here.

MAX. I did. I made a deal.

HORST. Sure. (HORST *rises & crosses left corner of right wall. Starts to leave again*)

MAX. They said if I . . . I could . . . they said . . .

HORST. (HORST *takes a step in toward* MAX) What?

MAX. Nothing. I could prove . . . I don't know how . . .

HORST. What? (*Stops, sits next to* MAX)

MAX. Nothing.

(*Silence.*)

HORST. (HORST *moves in to* MAX *and kneels to him*) Try.

(*Silence.*)

I think you better.

(*Silence.*)

Try to tell me.

MAX. Nothing.

(*Silence.*)

HORST. O.K. (HORST *stands to leave. Moves away*)

MAX. I made . . .

(MAX *pulls* HORST *down. The next lines do not relate to* HORST. *He finds it exceptionally difficult to tell.*)

they took me . . . into that room . . .

HORST. (*Stops*) Where?

MAX. Into that room.

HORST. On the train?

MAX. On the train. And they said . . . prove that you're . . . and I did . . .

HORST. Prove that you're what?

MAX. Not.

HORST. Not what?

MAX. Queer.

HORST. How?

MAX. Her.

HORST. Her?

MAX. They said, if you . . . and I did . . .

HORST. Did what?

MAX. Her. Made . . .

HORST. Made what?

MAX. Love.

HORST. Who to?

MAX. Her.

HORST. Who was she?

MAX. Only . . . maybe . . . maybe only thirteen . . . she was maybe . . . she was dead.

HORST. Oh.

MAX. Just. Just dead, minutes . . . (MAX *indicates a gun at the temple*) bullet . . . in her . . . they said . . . prove that you're . . . and I did . . . prove that you're . . . lots of them, watching . . . laughing . . . drinking . . . he's a bit bent, they said, he can't . . . but I did . . .

HORST. How?

MAX. I don't . . . I don't . . . know. I wanted . . .

HORST. To stay alive.

MAX. And there was something . . . (MAX *holds his head in his hands*)

HORST. Something . . .

MAX. Exciting . . . (MAX *raises his head*)

HORST. Oh God.

MAX. I hit him, you know. I kissed her. Dead lips. I killed him. Sweet lips. Angel.

HORST. God.

MAX. Angel . . . She was . . . like an angel . . . to save my life . . . little breasts just beginning . . . her breasts . . . just beginning . . . they said he can't . . . he's a bit bent . . . but I did . . . and I proved . . . I proved that I wasn't . . .
(*Silence.*)
And they enjoyed it.

HORST. Yes.

MAX. And I said, I'm not queer. And they laughed. And I said, give me a yellow star. And they said, sure make him a Jew. He's not bent. And they laughed. They were having fun. But . . . I . . . got . . . my . . . star . . . (MAX *fingers his star*)

HORST. (*Gently*) Oh yes.

MAX. I got my star.

HORST. Yes. (HORST *reaches for* MAX)

MAX. *Don't do that!* (MAX *pulls away right*) You mustn't do that. For your own sake. You mustn't touch me. I'm a rotten person.

HORST. No . . .

(HORST *reaches for* MAX *again.* MAX *strikes out at and crawls right.*)

MAX. Rotten.

> (HORST *stares at* MAX)

HORST. No.

(HORST *pauses then stands. He exits between walls and out UC. There is a silence.* MAX *leans against wall. He closes his eyes, takes a deep breath.*)

MAX. One. Two. Three. Four. Five. (MAX *takes another breath*) Six. Seven. Eight. Nine. Ten.

BLACKOUT

END OF ACT ONE.

ACT TWO

Scene One

One month later.

*A large fence extends across the stage. On front of the
fence, on one side, lies a pile of rocks. On the other
side—far over—a deep pit.*

MAX *is at SL rock pile*

MAX *crosses L pile—picks up rock.*

MAX *crosses R pile with rock*

MAX *crosses L pile*

When MAX *is at C,* GUARD *and* HORST *enter UL. The*
GUARD *crosses MLC and* HORST *is left of* GUARD.
The GUARD *stomps his foot when in position.*

GUARD. Here. You will work here.
         (MAX *crosses to left pile.*)
HORST. Yes sir.
GUARD. He'll explain.
HORST. Yes sir.
GUARD. I'm up there. (GUARD *points off UL*)
HORST. Yes sir.
    (MAX *picks up rock & crosses right.*)
GUARD. I see everything.
HORST. Yes sir.
GUARD. No laying about.
HORST. No sir.
  (MAX *begins to cross left but gets only MLC.*)

GUARD. I see everything.
HORST. Yes sir.
GUARD. (*To* MAX) You.

(MAX *stops MLC & stiffens to attention.* MAX *faces right and places rock right of himself.* GUARD *crosses USR of* MAX *and speaks to his head.*)

MAX. (*Puts down his rock*) Yes sir.
GUARD. Tell him what to do.
MAX. Yes sir.
GUARD. No laying about.
MAX. No sir.
GUARD. I see everything.
MAX. Yes sir.
GUARD. (*To* HORST) You.

(GUARD *crosses USL of* HORST *and speaks over* HORST'S *shoulder.*)

HORST. Yes sir.
GUARD. There are rest periods.
HORST. Yes sir.
GUARD. For three minutes.
HORST. Yes sir.
GUARD. Stand at attention.
HORST. Yes sir.
GUARD. Don't move.
HORST. No sir.
GUARD. Rest.
HORST. Yes sir.
GUARD. Three minutes.
HORST. Yes sir.
GUARD. A horn sounds.
HORST. Yes sir.
GUARD. (*To* MAX) You.
                (GUARD *crosses left of* MAX.)
MAX. Yes sir.

LIBRARY--F.K.C.C.

GUARD. Explain it to him.

MAX. Yes sir.

GUARD. No laying about.

MAX. No sir.

GUARD. (*To* HORST. GUARD *crosses UL of* HORST) You.

HORST. Yes sir.

GUARD. When the horn sounds.

HORST. Yes sir.

GUARD. Don't move.

HORST. No sir.

GUARD. Three minutes.

HORST. Yes sir.

GUARD. He'll explain.

HORST. Yes sir.

GUARD. (*To* MAX. GUARD *crosses right of* MAX *so face to face*) You.

MAX. Yes sir.

GUARD. You're responsible.

MAX. Yes sir.

GUARD. I'm up there.

MAX. Yes sir.

GUARD. (*To* HORST) You. (GUARD *crosses UL of* HORST)

HORST. Yes sir.

GUARD. I see everything.

HORST. Yes sir.

(GUARD *exits UL.*)

HORST. (HORST *looks left, & relaxes when* GUARD *is out of sight*) We had a kid like that in school.

(MAX *crosses right with rock.*)

Used to lead us in Simon Says.

MAX. O.K. I'll explain.

HORST. O.K.

MAX. (MAX *crosses left pile*) Hey — we can't stand here. We have to move rocks.

HORST. Yes sir. (HORST *crosses two steps left toward left pile.*)

MAX. You see those . . .

HORST. Yes sir.

MAX. You take one rock at a time.

HORST. Yes sir.

MAX. And move it over there. (MAX *points right*)

HORST. Yes sir.

MAX. And then when the entire pile is over there, (MAX *points right*) you take one rock at a time, and move it back. (MAX *points both arms to left pile and then picks up rock and crosses right.*)

(HORST *looks at* MAX. *Silence.*)

HORST. And move it back? (HORST *points left*)

MAX. Yes, (MAX *crosses right with rock.*)

HORST. We move the rocks from there to there, (HORST *points left*) and then back from there (HORST *points right*) to there? (HORST *points left*)

MAX. Yes sir.

HORST. *Why?*

MAX. Start moving. He's watching.

(MAX *watches* HORST *pick up rock.* MAX *crosses to left pile and* HORST *crosses to right pile, D.S. of* MAX.)

HORST. O.K.

(HORST & MAX *meet C.*)

MAX. It's supposed to drive us crazy.

HORST. These are heavy! (HORST *crosses to right pile, deposits rock; crosses left*)

MAX. You get used to it.

HORST. What do you mean, drive us crazy?

MAX. Just that. (MAX *crosses right, DS of* HORST.) It makes no sense. It serves no purpose. I figured it out. They do it to drive us crazy.

(HORST *crosses left with rock.* MAX *crosses left.*)

HORST. They probably know what they're doing. (HORST *reaches pile right*)
MAX. But it doesn't work.
(HORST *crosses left pile.*)
I figured it out. (*Pause.* MAX *crosses right*) It's the best job in the camp.
(*Pause.* MAX *crosses left,* HORST *crosses right.*)
That's why I got you here.
(*They meet at center*)
HORST. *What?* (HORST *stops MRC*)
MAX. Don't stop. Keep moving.
(HORST *crosses right pile with rock.*)
A couple more things. That fence.

(MAX *crosses right US of* HORST. HORST *crosses left.*)

HORST. Yes.
(*They meet at center.*)
MAX. It's electric. Don't touch it. You fry.
HORST. I won't touch it.
MAX. And over there — that pit.
HORST. Where?
MAX. There. (MAX *straightens rocks*)
HORST. Oh yes. (HORST *crosses right pile with rock*) It smells awful. (HORST *deposits rock & kneels*)
MAX. Bodies.
HORST. In the pit.
MAX. Yes. Sometimes we have to throw them in. (MAX *crosses left of pile*)
HORST. Oh. Well, it will break the routine. (HORST *rises, crosses left quickly to get behind* MAX) What do you mean you got me here?
MAX. Don't walk so fast. (MAX *crosses right with rock, DS of* HORST.)
HORST. Why?

MAX. You'll tire yourself. Pace it. Nice and slow.

(HORST *crosses right as step'n fetchit*.)

HORST. O.K. This better? (HORST *gets MRC*)
MAX. Yeah. (MAX *crosses left*)

(HORST *places rock on right pile and then crosses left behind* MAX.)

HORST. What do you mean you got me here?
MAX. I worked a deal. (MAX *picks up rock; crosses right*)
HORST. I don't want to hear.
                    (*Silence.*)
Yes, I do. (HORST *picks up rock; crosses right quickly to get behind* MAX) What the hell is this? You *got* me here? What right do you have . . .
MAX. Careful. (MAX *drops his rock on pile*)
HORST. What?
MAX. You drop the rock.
HORST. (HORST *holds rock in DS hand only*) No I won't.
                    (MAX *drops rock on pile*.)
I'm holding it, I'm holding it.
        (HORST *drops rock on pile;* MAX *crosses left*.)
What right do you have . . .
            (HORST *follows* MAX *right behind him*.)
MAX. You were at the stones?
HORST. Yes.
MAX. Was work harder than this?
HORST. I guess.
MAX. People get sick?
HORST. Yes.
MAX. Die?
HORST. Yes.
MAX. Guards beat you if you didn't work hard enough?

HORST. Yes.

MAX. (*Proudly*) So? (MAX *picks up rock*)

HORST. So? So what?

MAX. (MAX *crosses right*) So it was dangerous.

HORST. This isn't?

MAX. No. No one gets sick here.

(MAX *gets MRC rock;* HORST *picks up rock and crosses to right pile.* MAX *crosses to left pile.*)

Look at all those guys moving rocks over there.

(*They meet H-RC,* MAX *points out L in audience. They stop—*MAX *L of C, & R of C of* HORST.)

They look healthier than most. (MAX *crosses to left pile*) No one dies. The guards

(HORST *crosses to right pile.*)

don't beat you, because the work is totally non-essential.

(MAX *crosses right with rock;* HORST *crosses left*)

All it can do is drive you crazy.

HORST. That's all?

MAX. Yes.

HORST. Then maybe the other was better.

MAX. No, I figured it out!

(HORST *crosses right with rock,* MAX *US of pile straightening rock.*)

This is the best work in the camp, if you keep your head, if you have someone to talk to.

HORST. Ah! I see! Someone to talk to! Don't you think you should have asked me . . .

MAX. Asked you what?

HORST. If I wanted to move rocks, if I wanted to talk to you . . .

MAX. Didn't have a chance. They moved you.

HORST. Thank heaven.

MAX. Your new barracks, is it all pink triangles?

HORST. Yes. They're arresting more queers each day; they keep pouring into the camp. Is yours all yellow stars now?

MAX. Yes.

HORST. Good. You might go all religious. There was an old man at the stones. A rabbi. Really kind. It's not easy being kind here. He was. I thought of you.

MAX. Why?

HORST. Maybe if you knew him you could be proud of your star. You should be proud of *something*.

(*Silence.*)

MAX. Don't keep looking at me. As long as they don't see us look at each other they can't tell we're talking.

(*Silence.*)

HORST. Where do the bodies come from?

MAX. What bodies?

HORST. The ones in the pit.

MAX. The fence. The hat trick.

HORST. Oh. What's that?

MAX. Sometimes a guard throws a prisoner's hat on the fence. He orders him to get the hat. If he doesn't get the hat, the guard will shoot him. If he does get the hat, he'll be electrocuted. (MAX *crosses left*)

HORST. I'm really going to like it here. Thanks a lot.

MAX. I'm really doing you a favor.

HORST. (HORST *crosses left*) Some favor! You just want someone to talk to

(MAX *picks up rock*)

so you won't go crazy. And I'm the only one who knows your secret.

MAX. What secret?

HORST. (HORST *picks up rock and crosses right behind* MAX) That you're a pink triangle.

MAX. No. I'm a Jew now.

HORST. You are not.

MAX. They think I am.

HORST. But it's a lie.

MAX. It's a smart lie.

HORST. You're crazy.

MAX. I thought you'd be grateful.

(HORST *overtakes* MAX.)

HORST. That's why you like this job. It can't drive you crazy. You're already there. (HORST *crosses US of left pile*)

MAX. I spent money getting you here.

HORST. Money?

MAX. Yes. (MAX *crosses right with rock*) I bribed the guard.

HORST. Where'd you get money? (HORST *crosses right with rock*)

MAX. My uncle sent me some.

HORST. And you bribed the guard?

MAX. Yes.

HORST. For me?

MAX. Yes. (MAX *crosses left.*)

HORST. Used *your* money? (HORST *crosses left.*)

MAX. Yes.

HORST. You'll probably never get money again.

MAX. Probably not.

(*Beat.*)

HORST. You are crazy. (HORST *picks up rock and crosses right with rock*)

MAX. I thought you'd be grateful.

HORST. You should have asked me first.

MAX. How could I ask you. We're in separate barracks. Do you think it's easy to bribe a guard? (MAX *crosses left US of pile*) It's complicated. It's dangerous. He could have turned on me. I took a risk. Do you think I didn't?

(HORST *crosses right with rock*)

I took a risk. I thought you'd be grateful.

HORST. I'm *not* grateful. I like cutting stones. I liked that old rabbi. This is insane. (HORST *crosses left*)

Twelve hours of this a day? I'll be nuts in a week. Like you. Jesus! (HORST *crosses right with rock*)

MAX. I'm sorry I did it.

HORST. *You're* sorry? (HORST *crosses left*)

MAX. You haven't figured out this camp, (MAX *crosses right with rock*) that's all. You don't know what's good for you. This is the best work in the camp.

HORST. (HORST *picks up rock*) Moving rocks back and forth for no reason. Next to a pit with dead bodies and a fence that can burn you to dust. The *best* job to have?

(HORST *crosses left,* MAX *follows.*)

MAX. *Yes.* You don't understand.

HORST. I don't want to understand. I don't want to talk to you.

(*Pause.*)
(HORST *crosses right,* MAX *follows him right.*)

MAX. You have to talk to me.

HORST. Why?

(HORST *crosses left,* MAX *follows* HORST *left.*)
(*Pause.*)

MAX. I got you here to talk.

HORST. (HORST *crosses right*) Well, tough. I don't want to talk. Move your rocks, and I'll move mine. Just don't speak to me.

(*They both move their rocks.*)
(*A long silence.*)
(MAX *crosses right,* HORST *crosses left.* MAX *crosses left,* HORST *crosses right.*)

MAX. I thought you'd be grateful.

BLACKOUT

End of Scene One.

ACT II

Scene Two

(*The same. Three days later.*)

(MAX *and* HORST *are moving rocks. It is very hot. Their shirts lie on the ground.*)

(*A long silence.*)

(MAX *crosses left with rock,* HORST *crosses right.*)

HORST. It's so hot.
MAX. Yes.
HORST. Burning hot.
MAX. Yes.

(MAX *crosses right;* HORST *crosses left with rock.*)

(*Silence.*)

MAX. (MAX *stops MRC*) You talked to me. (MAX *crosses to right pile*)
HORST. Weather talk, that's all.

(MAX *crosses left with rock;* HORST *crosses right.*)

MAX. After three days of silence.
HORST. *Weather* talk.
          (*Meet C,* MAX *US of* HORST.)
Everyone talks about the weather.
          (*Silence.*)
(HORST *crosses left with rock;* MAX *crosses right. They pass C.*)
Anyhow.
          (*Silence.*)
MAX. (MAX *at right rock pile*) Did you say something?

HORST. No.

(MAX *crosses left with rock,* HORST *crosses right.*)

(*Silence.*)

HORST. Anyhow.

MAX. Anyhow?

HORST. (HORST *stands still at right rock pile*) Anyhow.

(MAX *crosses to right rock pile.*)

Anyhow, I'm sorry. (*Stands still*) Sometimes in this place, I behave like everyone else — bloody awful. Cut off, mean, not human, I'm sorry.

(MAX *crosses left with rock.*)

You were doing me a favour. This is a good place to be. And the favour won't work unless we talk, will it?

MAX. (MAX *at left pile*) *Move!*

HORST. What?

MAX. (MAX *crosses right*) Talk while you're moving. Don't stop.

(HORST *crosses left with rock,* HORST *US of* MAX.)

They can see us.

HORST. (*Starts to move the rock again*) It's hard to talk when you're going one way and I'm going the other. God, it's hot.

(HORST *crosses right,* MAX *crosses left with rock.*)

(*Silence.*)

(HORST *and* MAX *meet C.*)

HORST. Somebody died last night.

MAX. Where?

HORST. In my barracks. A moslem.

MAX. An Arab?

HORST. No.

(HORST *crosses left with rock,* MAX *waiting at left pile.*)

A moslem. That's what they call a dead person who walks. You know, one of those guys who won't eat

anymore, won't talk anymore, just wanders around
waiting to really die.
                    (*They meet at left pile.*)
   MAX. I've seen them. (MAX *crosses right*)
   HORST. So one really died.
           (HORST *crosses right, follows* MAX.)
In my barracks.
                        (*Silence.*)
       (HORST *DS of* MAX *at right pile, squatting.*)
God, it's hot.
                        (*Silence.*)
   MAX. We'll miss the Olympics.
   (MAX *picks up rock, crosses 2 steps SL of* HORST.)
   HORST. The *what?*
           (HORST *speaks over shoulder to* MAX.)
   MAX. Olympics. Next month in Berlin.
   HORST. I knew there was a reason I didn't want to be
here.
   MAX. (MAX *starts left*) Maybe they'll release us.
   HORST. (HORST *rises*) for the Olympics?

       (*They cross left,* HORST *behind* MAX.)

   MAX. As a good will gesture. (MAX *crosses right*) It is
possible, don't you think.
   HORST. (HORST *crosses right*) I think it's hot.
                        (*Silence.*)
   MAX. (MAX *crosses left*) Heard a rumor.
   HORST. What?
   MAX. We get sardines tonight.
   HORST. I don't like sardines.
   MAX. It's only a rumor. (MAX *at right pile*)
                        (*Silence.*)
   HORST. (HORST *at left with rock*) God, it's hot.
                        (*Silence.*)
   MAX. Sure is. (MAX *crosses left with rock*)
                (HORST *crosses right.*)

(*Silence.*)
(*They pass C.*)

HORST. Sure is what?
(*Silence.*)
(MAX *at L,* HORST *at R.*)

MAX. Sure is hot.
(*Silence.*)

HORST. Suppose . . .
(*Silence.*)

MAX. What?
(*Silence.*)
(HORST *starts L,* MAX *starts R.*)

HORST. Suppose after all of this . . .
(*Silence.*)
We have nothing to talk about.

(*Horn sounds —* HORST *at LC puts rock on ground;* MAX *at RC.*)

HORST. Shit! I'd rather be moving rocks than standing in the sun. (*Pause*) Some rest period.
MAX. It's part of their plan.
HORST. What plan.
MAX. To drive us crazy.
(*Silence.*)
Was I awful to bring you here?
HORST. No.
MAX. I was, wasn't I?
HORST. No.
MAX. I had no right . . .
HORST. Stop it. Stop thinking how awful you are. Come on, don't get depressed. Smile.
(*Silence.*)
You're not smiling.
MAX. You can't see me.
HORST. I can feel you.
MAX. I wish we could look at each other.

HORST. I can feel you.

MAX. They hate it if anyone looks at each other.

HORST. I snuck a glance.

MAX. At what?

HORST. At you.

MAX. When?

HORST. Before.

MAX. Yeah?

HORST. A couple of glances. You look sexy.

MAX. Me?

HORST. Without your shirt.

MAX. No.

HORST. Come off it. You know you're sexy.

MAX. No.

HORST. Liar.

MAX. (MAX *smiles*) Of course I'm a liar.

HORST. Sure.

MAX. I've always been sexy.

HORST. Hu huh.

MAX. Since I was a kid.

HORST. Yes?

MAX. Twelve. I got into a lot of trouble when I was . . .

HORST. Twelve?

MAX. Twelve.

HORST. Your body's beautiful.

MAX. I take care of it. I exercise.

HORST. What?

MAX. At night I do pushups and knee bends in the barracks. After I get home from work.

HORST. After twelve hours of moving rocks?

MAX. Sure. I figured it out. You got to keep your entire body strong. By yourself. That's how you survive here. You should do it.

HORST. I don't like to exercise.

MAX. But you're a nurse.

HORST. For other people, not myself.

MAX. Still you have to think of survival.

HORST. Sleep. I think of sleep. That's how I survive.
Or I think of nothing.

(*Silence.*)

That scares me. When I think of nothing.

(*Silence.*)

MAX. Your body's nice too.

HORST. It's O.K. Not great.

MAX. No, it's nice.

HORST. Not as nice as yours.

MAX. No. But it's O.K.

(*Both laugh.*)

HORST. How do you know?

MAX. I looked. I snuck a few glances too.

HORST. When?

MAX. All day.

HORST. Yes?

MAX. Yes.

(*Silence.*)

HORST. Listen, do you . . .

MAX. What?

HORST. Miss . . .

MAX. What?

HORST. You know.

MAX. No I don't.

HORST. Everyone misses it.

MAX. No.

HORST. Everyone in the camp.

MAX. No.

HORST. They go crazy missing it.

MAX. No.

HORST. Come on. No one can hear us. You're not a
yellow star with me, remember? Do you miss it?

MAX. I don't want . . .

HORST. What?

MAX. To miss it.

HORST. But do you?

(*Silence.*)

MAX. Yes.

HORST. Me too.

(*Silence.*)

We don't have to.

MAX. What?

HORST. Miss it.

(*Silence.*)

We're here together. We don't have to miss it.

MAX. We can't look at each other. We can't touch.

HORST. We can feel . . .

MAX. Feel what?

HORST. Each other. Without looking. Without touching. I can feel you right now. Next to me. Can you feel me?

MAX. No.

HORST. No one can hear us. Come on. Don't be afraid. Can you feel me?

MAX. Maybe.

HORST. It's alright. No one's going to know. Feel me.

MAX. Maybe.

HORST. Feel me.

MAX. It's so hot.

HORST. I'm touching you.

MAX. No.

HORST. I'm touching you.

MAX. It's burning.

HORST. I'm kissing you.

MAX. Burning.

HORST. Kissing your eyes.

MAX. Yes.

HORST. Kissing your lips.

MAX. Yes.

HORST. Mouth.

MAX. Yes.

HORST. Inside your mouth.
MAX. Yes.
HORST. Neck.
MAX. Yes.
HORST. Down . . .
MAX. Yes.
HORST. Down . . .
MAX. Yes.
HORST. Chest. My tongue . . .
MAX. Burning.
HORST. Your chest.
MAX. Your mouth.
HORST. I'm kissing your chest.
MAX. Yes.
HORST. Hard.
MAX. Yes.
HORST. Down . . .
MAX. Yes.
HORST. Down . . .
MAX. Yes.
HORST. Your cock.
MAX. Yes.
HORST. Do you feel my mouth?
MAX. Yes. Do you feel my cock?
HORST. Yes. Do you feel . . .
MAX. Do you feel . . .
HORST. Mouth.
MAX. Cock.
HORST. Cock.
MAX. Mouth.
HORST. Do you feel my cock?
MAX. Do you feel my mouth?
HORST. Yes.
MAX. Do you know what I'm doing?
HORST. Yes. Can you taste what I'm doing?
MAX. Yes.

HORST. Taste.

MAX. Feel.

HORST. Together . . .

MAX. Together . . .

HORST. Do you feel me?

MAX. I feel you.

HORST. I see you.

MAX. I feel you.

HORST. I have you.

MAX. I want you.

HORST. Do you feel me inside you?

MAX. I want you inside me.

HORST. Feel . . .

MAX. I have you inside me.

HORST. Inside . . .

MAX. Strong.

HORST. Do you feel me thrust . . .

MAX. Hold.

HORST. Stroke . . .

MAX. Strong . . .

HORST. Oh . . .

MAX. Strong . . .

HORST. Oh . . .

MAX. Strong . . .

HORST. I'm going to . . .

MAX. Strong . . .

HORST. Do you feel . . . I'm going to . . .

MAX. I feel us both.

HORST. Do you . . .

MAX. Oh yes . . .

HORST. Do you . . .

MAX. Yes. Yes.

HORST. Feel . . .

MAX. Yes. Strong . . .

HORST. Feel . . .

MAX. More . . .

HORST. Ohh . . .

MAX. Now . . .

HORST. Yes . . .

MAX. Now! (*Gasps*) Oh! Oh! My God! (*Has orgasm*)

HORST. Ohh! . . . Now! Ohh! . . . (*Has orgasm*)

(*Silence.*)

HORST. Oh.

(*Silence.*)

HORST. Did you?

MAX. Yes. *You?*

HORST. Yes.

(*Silence.*)

MAX. You're a good lay.

HORST. So are you.

(*Silence.*)

MAX. It's awfully sticky.

(*Silence.*)

HORST. Max?

MAX. What?

HORST. We did it. How about that — fucking guards, fucking camp, we did it.

MAX. Don't shout.

HORST. O.K. But I'm shouting inside. We did it. They're not going to kill us. We made love. We were real. We were human. We made love. They're not going to kill us.

(*Silence.*)

MAX. I never . . .

HORST. What?

MAX. Thought we'd . . .

HORST. What?

MAX. Do it in three minutes.

(*They laugh. The horn sounds. They pick up their rocks and resume moving them from one side to the other.*)

BLACKOUT

End of Scene Two

ACT II

Scene Three

(*The same. Two months later.*)

(HORST *at LC at attention.* MAX *at RC at attention —
DS of him.*)

HORST. I'm going crazy.
> (*Silence.*)

I'm going crazy.
> (*Silence.*)

I'm going crazy. I dream about rocks. I close my eyes
and I'm moving rocks. Rocks never end. Never end.
> (*Silence.*)

I'm going crazy.

MAX. Think of something else.

HORST. I can't think. I've been up all night. *That's*
why I'm going crazy.

MAX. Up all night?

HORST. Come on, didn't you hear. Our barracks had
to stand outside all night.

MAX. No.

HORST. Yes. We stood at attention all night long.
Punishment.

MAX. For what?

HORST. Someone in our barracks killed himself.

MAX. A moslem?

HORST. Of course not. It doesn't mean anything if a
moslem kills himself but if a person who's still a person

commits suicide, well . . . it's a kind of defiance, isn't it?
They hate that — it's an act of free will.

MAX. I'm sorry.

HORST. Sure. Yellow star is sorry.

(*Silence.*)

MAX. Heard a rumor.

HORST. What?

MAX. Sardines tonight.

HORST. I hate sardines! I hate all food. Scraps. Sardine scraps. That's all we get anyhow. Not worth eating.
Didn't know you could have sardine scraps.

(*Silence.*)

I'm going crazy.

MAX. O.K. O.K. You're going crazy. I'm sorry. It's
my fault.

HORST. What do you mean *your* fault?

MAX. For bringing you here. Because you make me
feel so guilty. And you should. This job *is* the worst. I
figured it wrong. I'm sorry.

HORST. I'm glad to be here.

MAX. Oh sure.

HORST. I am.

MAX. How can you be?

HORST. That's my secret. (*2 Beats*)

(*Pause. Horn sounds.* MAX *starts to move rocks.*
    HORST *remains still.* MAX *picks up rock. US*
    HORST.*)

HORST. Maybe if I closed my eyes . . .

(MAX *pushes* HORST *to R.*)

MAX. Heard a rumor.

HORST. What? (*Starts to move rocks*)

MAX. We may get potatoes.

HORST. When?

MAX. Tomorrow.

HORST. I don't believe it.

MAX. They said so in my barracks. (MAX *crosses L*)

HORST. Who's they? (HORST *crosses L*)

MAX. Some guys.

HORST. Are they cute?

      (MAX *turns R to* HORST.)

MAX. Cut it out.

(HORST *laughs.* MAX *crosses L continues,* HORST continues L.)

HORST. You should be with us,

      (MAX *crosses R with rock.*)

where you belong.

MAX. No.

      (HORST *crosses R with rock.*)

But you shouldn't be *here.*

HORST. I want to be here.

MAX. Why would you want to be here — are you crazy? (MAX *crosses L*)

HORST. Of course I'm crazy. (HORST *crosses L*) I'm trying to tell you I'm crazy. And I want to be here.

MAX. Why? (MAX *crosses R with rock*)

HORST. Because. Because I love rocks.

(MAX *crosses L,* HORST *crosses R with rock. Pause. They meet C.*)

Because I love you.

      (*Silence.*)

I do. I love you.

      (HORST *crosses L, US of* MAX. MAX *crosses R.*)

When I'm not dreaming about rocks, I'm dreaming about you. For the past six weeks, I've dreamt about you. (HORST *crosses twice*) It helps me get up. It helps me make sure my bed is perfectly made so I'm not punished. It helps me eat the stinking food.

      (MAX *straightens rocks.*)

It helps me put up with the constant fights in the barracks. Knowing I'll see you. (HORST *crosses R with*

rock) At least out of the corner of my eyes. In passing.
It's a reason to live. So I'm glad I'm here.

(MAX *US of R pile.*)

HORST. What are you doing?

MAX. Arranging these neatly. We've gotten sloppy.
They can beat you for it.

(*Silence.* HORST *crosses L.*)

(MAX *crosses L, US of* HORST.)

(MAX *holds* HORST *by shoulder L.*)

Don't love me. (MAX *crosses to L pile*)

HORST. (HORST *crosses to L pile*) It makes me happy.
It doesn't harm anyone. It's my secret.

MAX. I don't want anyone to love me.

HORST. It's my secret. And I have a signal.

(MAX *crosses L,* HORST *crosses R with rock.*)

No one knows it.

(*They meet C.*)

When I rub my left eyebrow at you, like this . . .(*Rubs
his left eyebrow*) it means I love you. Bet you didn't
know that.

(HORST *crosses L,* MAX *crosses R with rock, DL of pile.*)
I can even do it in front of the guards. (HORST *crosses R
with rock*) No one knows. It's my secret. (HORST *starts
to cough*) It's cold. It was better hot. I don't like it cold.

MAX. Don't love me.

(HORST *crosses L*)

HORST. I can't help it.

MAX. I don't want anybody to love me.

HORST. Too bad.

MAX. I can't love anybody back.

(*Pause.*)

HORST. Who's asking you to?

MAX. Queers aren't meant to love. I know. I thought
I loved someone once. He worked in my father's factory. My father paid him to go away. He went. Queers
aren't meant to love.

(MAX *crosses L;* HORST *crosses L, follows* MAX.)
They don't want us to.
  (MAX *turns R to* HORST, *and picks up rock.*)
You know who loved me? Than dancer. I don't
remember his name. But I killed him. See — queers
aren't meant to love. (MAX *crosses R with rock*)
   (HORST *crosses R with rock.*)
    (MAX *turn to* HORST.)
I'll kill you too. Hate me. That's better. Hate me. Don't
love me.
   (MAX *crosses L,* HORST *deposits rock.*)
 HORST. I'll do what I want to do.
   (HORST *crosses L,* MAX *crosses R with rock.*)
It isn't any of your business, anyhow. I'm sorry I told
you.
    (MAX *kicks rocks.*)
 MAX. I'm sorry I brought you here.
    (HORST *crosses R with rock.*)
     (*Silence.*)
     (HORST *coughs.*)
   (HORST *crosses L,* MAX *crosses R.*)
 MAX. Why are you coughing?
 HORST. Because I like to.
 MAX. Are you catching cold?
 HORST. Probably. Up all night. In the wind.
   (MAX *crosses L,* HORST *crosses R with rock.*)
 MAX. Winter's coming.
 HORST. I know.
     (*Silence.*)
I just want to close my eyes . . .
    (MAX *crosses R with rock.*)
 MAX. (MAX *shout loudly*) Heard a rumor.
 HORST. (HORST *crosses L*) I don't care.

(MAX *crosses L, gets ¾ across before* HORST *drops
 rock.*)

MAX. Don't you want to hear it?

(HORST *picks up rock & crosses 2 steps to C on trip R.*)

HORST. Stuff your rumors. (HORST *coughs.* HORST *drops rock & collapses on ground, kneels*)

MAX. Horst!

HORST. Shit.

(MAX *crosses R of* HORST.)

Don't move! He's watching. The guard. Don't help me. If you help me, they'll kill you. Get back to your rock. Do you hear me, get back!

(MAX *returns, picks up his rock, but stands looking at* HORST; HORST *is coughing — looks up at* MAX.)

Move!

(MAX *crosses R of pile, gets rock.*)

(MAX *crosses to L pile.*)

Right. I'm O.K. I'll get up.

(MAX *crosses R.*)

I'll get up. Don't ever help me. (HORST *stands*) I'm up. It's O.K.

(HORST *picks up rock,* MAX *crosses L.*)

These bloody things get heavier and heavier. (HORST *crosses L*) The guard was watching.

(MAX *follows* HORST *left*)

He'd kill you if you helped me.

(HORST *picks up rock & turns R to confront* MAX *face to face.*)

Never notice. Never watch. (HORST *continues R*) Remember? I love you. But I won't help you if *you* fall. Don't you dare help me. You don't even love me, so why are you going to help?

(HORST *crosses L,* MAX *crosses R with rock.*)

(HORST *crosses R with rock,* MAX *crosses L.*)

We save *ourselves.* Do you understand? Do you?

MAX. Yes. I understand.

HORST. (HORST *crosses L to C*) Promise me. Come on. Promise me. We save ourselves.
MAX. O.K. (MAX *crosses R to C*)
HORST. Promise me!

(*They meet face to face C.*)

(MAX *tries to step aside &* HORST *blocks with leg.*)

MAX. *YES!*

' (HORST *crosses L,* MAX *looks at* HORST.)

HORST. (HORST *crosses R with rock*) You're a fool. I don't love you anymore. (HORST *crosses L*)
    (MAX *crosses R with rock, continues.*)
It was just a passing fancy. I love myself.
    (HORST *crosses R with rock,* MAX *crosses L.*)
Poor you, you don't love anybody.
       (*Silence.*)
      (HORST *coughs.*)
    (HORST *crosses L,* MAX *crosses R with rock.*)
It's getting cold. Winter's coming.
    (*They walk, moving the rocks, in silence.*)

BLACKOUT

End of Scene Three

ACT TWO

Scene Four

(*The same. Two months later.*)

(HORST *crosses to R pile.*)

(MAX *at L pile.*)

(HORST *crosses to R pile & coughs.*)

MAX. (MAX *crosses R with rock*) You have a barracks leader.

(HORST'S *coughing continues.*)

He can get you medicine. (MAX *crosses L*)

(*Coughing continues.*)

He can try to get you medicine.

(HORST *crosses L, falls C, coughing continues.*)

You have to ask him.

(*Coughing continues.*)

You have to get help. (MAX *crosses RC*)

(*Coughing continues.*)

You have to stop coughing — damn it. (MAX *crosses to R pile*)

(*The coughing spell slowly subsides.*)

HORST. It doesn't matter.

MAX. If you're nice to the kapo . . .

HORST. It doesn't matter.

MAX. Some sort of medicine.

HORST. What for? The cough? How about the hands?

MAX. I told you what to do. Exercise.

HORST. They're frostbitten.

MAX. (MAX *crosses L with rock*) So exercise.

HORST. It doesn't matter.

MAX. Every night, (MAX *crosses R*) I move my fingers up and down, one at a time, for a half hour. I don't do pushups anymore. Just fingers.

HORST. (HORST *rises, crosses L*) It doesn't matter. (HORST *crosses L with rock*)

MAX. You're losing weight. (MAX *crosses L*)

HORST. I don't like sardines.

(MAX *crosses R.*)

(HORST *coughs at L pile.*)

MAX. (MAX *crosses L with rock*) It's getting worse.

HORST. It's getting colder.

MAX. (MAX *crosses L*) You need medicine.
HORST. (HORST *crosses R*) Stop nagging me.
MAX. See your kapo.
HORST. He doesn't care.
     (MAX *crosses R in front of* HORST.)
MAX. Ask him.
HORST. He wants money.

  (MAX *stops RC. He knows how to get money.*)

MAX. Are you sure? (MAX *crosses R to pile*)
HORST. It doesn't matter.

    (MAX *crosses SR of R pile to face* HORST.)

MAX. I thought you cared about yourself.
HORST. You don't know anything. (HORST *crosses L with rock*)
MAX. I thought you loved yourself.
HORST. It's too cold.
MAX. You know what?
(MAX *crosses L with rock to get ahead of* HORST *and to back into him.*)
You know what? You're turning into a moslem. (MAX *crosses L*) I'm scared.
HORST. Who isn't.

(MAX *crosses R, US of* HORST. HORST *crosses L, resumes crossing.*)

MAX. For you.
HORST. Be scared for yourself.
MAX. Why don't you listen to me?
HORST. Moslems don't listen.

  (HORST *crosses R;* MAX *crosses L with rock.*)

MAX. You're not a moslem.
HORST. You said I was.
MAX. I didn't mean it. You're not a moslem.

HORST. You're not a Jew.

MAX. Can't you ever forget that?

(HORST *crosses C;* MAX *crosses C.*)

HORST. If I forget that . . . then . . . I am a moslem.
(*The horn sounds.* HORST *puts down rock. They stand
    at attention.*)
Look, I'm just cold. My fingers are numb. I can't stop
coughing. I hate food. That's all. Nothing special.
Don't get upset.

MAX. I want you to care.

HORST. I would. If I was warm.

MAX. I'll warm you.

HORST. You can't.

MAX. I know how.

HORST. No. You don't.

MAX. I do. I'm terriffic at it. You said so.

HORST. When?

MAX. I'm next to you.

HORST. Don't start.

MAX. I'll make love to you.

HORST. Not now.

MAX. Yes. Now.

HORST. I have a headache. I can't.

MAX. Don't joke.

MAX. I'll make love to you.

HORST. No.

MAX. I'll make you warm.

                        (*Pause.*)

HORST. You can't.

MAX. You'll feel the warm . . .

HORST. I can't.

MAX. You'll *feel* it.

                        (*Pause.*)

HORST. In my fingers?

MAX. All over.

HORST. I can't.

MAX. I'm kissing your fingers.

HORST. They're numb.

MAX. My mouth is hot.

HORST. They're cold.

MAX. My mouth is on fire.

HORST. My fingers . . .

MAX. Are getting warm.

HORST. Are they?

MAX. They're getting warm.

HORST. I can't tell.

MAX. They're getting warm.

HORST. A little.

MAX. They're getting warm.

HORST. Yes.

MAX. My mouth is on fire. Your fingers are on fire. Your body's on fire.

HORST. Yes.

MAX. My mouth is all over you.

HORST. Yes.

MAX. My mouth is on your chest . . .

HORST. Yes.

MAX. Kissing your chest.

HORST. Yes.

MAX. Making it warm.

HORST. Yes.

MAX. Biting your nipple.

HORST. Yes.

MAX. Biting . . . into it . . .

HORST. Yes.

MAX. Harder . . . harder . . . harder . . .

HORST. Hold it! That hurts!

MAX. Harder . . .

HORST. No, hold it. I'm serious. You're hurting me.
        (*A pause.* MAX *catches his breath.*)

MAX. You pulled away.

HORST. Damn right.

MAX. It was exciting.

HORST. For *you* maybe. I don't try to hurt you.

MAX. I like being hurt. It's exciting.

HORST. It's not. Not when you're rough.

MAX. I'm not being rough.

HORST. Yes you are. Sometimes you are.

MAX. O.K. So what? It's exciting.

HORST. Why'd you have to spoil it? You were making me warm. Why can't you be gentle?

MAX. I am.

HORST. You're not. You try to hurt me. You make me warm, and then you hurt me. I hurt enough. I don't want to feel *more* pain. Why can't you be gentle?

MAX. I am.

HORST. No, you're not. You're like them. You're like the Gestapo. You're like the guards. We stopped being gentle. I watched it, when we were on the outside. People made pain and called it love. I don't want to be like that. You don't make love to hurt.

MAX. I wanted to make you warm. That's all I wanted. I can't do anything right. I don't understand you. I used to do things right.

HORST. You still can.

MAX. People liked it when I got rough. Not everybody. He didn't.

HORST. Who?

MAX. The dancer. But everyone else did. Just a little rough.

HORST. Did you like it?

MAX. I don't remember. I could never remember. I was always drunk. There was always cocaine. Nothing seemed to matter that much.

HORST. Some things do matter.

MAX. Not to you.

HORST. They do.

MAX. I don't understand you. All day long you've been saying nothing matters . . . your cough, your fingers . . .

HORST. They matter.

MAX. I don't understand anything anymore.

HORST. They matter. I'm not a moslem. You're not a Jew. My fingers are cold.

MAX. I want you to be happy.

HORST. Is that true?

MAX. I think so. I don't know (*Pause*) Yes.

HORST. Then be gentle with me.

MAX. I don't know how.

HORST. Just hold me.

MAX. I'm afraid to hold you.

HORST. Don't be.

MAX. I'm afraid.

HORST. Don't be.

MAX. I'm going to drown.

HORST. Hold me. Please. Hold me.

MAX. O.K. I'm holding you.

HORST. Are you?

MAX. Yes. You're in my arms.

HORST. Am I?

MAX. You're here in my arms. I promise. I'm holding you. You're here . . .

HORST. Touch me.

MAX. No.

HORST. Gently . . .

MAX. Here.

HORST. Are you?

MAX. Yes. Touching. Softly . . . I'm touching you softly . . . gently . . . you're safe . . . I'll keep you safe . . . and warm . . . you're with me now . . . you'll never be cold again . . . I'm holding you now . . . safe . . . and warm . . . as long as you're here, as long as you're with me, as long as I'm holding you, you're safe . . .

BLACKOUT

End of Scene Four

ACT TWO

Scene Five

(*The same. Three days later.*)

(MAX *is moving rocks.* HORST *is putting the rock pile into neat order.*)

HORST. The air is fresh today. Clean.

(MAX *hands* HORST *a needle and a thread, as he passes the rock pile.*)

(HORST *starts to cough — continues coughing — then stops.*)

MAX. It sounds better.
HORST. It does.
MAX. Loosening up.
HORST. It is.
MAX. The medicine is helping.
HORST. Yes. (*Silence*) Thank you. (*Silence*) Why don't you tell me.
MAX. Tell you what?
HORST. How you got it.
MAX. I told you. Spoke to my barracks leader. He took me to an officer.
HORST. Which one?
MAX. Some captain. The new one.
HORST. He's rotten.
MAX. You know him?

HORST. I've heard of him. You gave him money?

MAX. Yes.

HORST. Liar.

MAX. Why don't you ever believe me?

HORST. Because I can tell when you're lying. You think you're so terriffic at it. You're not. Your voice changes.

MAX. It *what?*

HORST. Changes. Sounds different.

MAX. Bullshit.

(MAX *crosses R with rock.* HORST *crosses L of rock pile to get rock.*)

(*Silence.*)

MAX. Hey . . .

(HORST *crosses behind* MAX.)

MAX. Guess who I saw?

HORST. Where?

(MAX *and* HORST *cross R.*)

MAX. In my barracks.

HORST. Marlene Dietrich.

MAX. No. My landlord. From Berlin. Rosen. (MAX *crosses L*)

HORST. Oh. (HORST *follows L*)

MAX. Nice man.

HORST. I thought you hated him.

MAX. Sure, I used to think he was what I was supposed to think he was.

HORST. What was that?

MAX. A lousy Jew. (MAX *crosses R with rock*)

HORST. He probably (HORST *follows R with rock*) thought you were a lousy queer.

MAX. Probably.

HORST. Now he thinks you're not a queer. He must be very confused. It's a shame.

MAX. (MAX *crosses L, US of* HORST) It's not a shame. Don't start in.

> (HORST *follows L.*)
> (HORST *coughs.*)

You *are* taking the medicine?

HORST. (*The coughing subsides*) Of course I am.

> (MAX *crosses R with rock.*)
> (*Silence.*)

Of course I am. Max.

> (MAX *stops C on R cross.*)

I'm glad you got it.

MAX. So am I. (MAX *crosses R with rock*)

> (*Silence.*)

HORST. Wish I knew how, though.

MAX. I told you.

HORST. You're a liar. (HORST *crosses R with rock*)

MAX. (MAX *crosses L*) You're never going to let up, are you?

HORST. Probably not.

MAX. Suppose you don't like the answer.

> (HORST *crosses L.*)

HORST. I'll chance it.

MAX. Then when I tell you, you'll nag me about *that*.

HORST. You chance it.

> (MAX *picks up rock—looks at* HORST.)

MAX. I went down on him. (MAX *crosses R with rock*)

HORST. What?

MAX. You heard me.

HORST. No I didn't.

MAX. I told you you wouldn't like it.

HORST. That SS captain?

MAX. Uh-huh.

HORST. (HORST *crosses R with rock*) You went down on him?

MAX. I had to. I didn't have any money.

HORST. (HORST *follows L*) You touched him?

MAX. No. I just went down on him. That's what he wanted. And I needed the medicine. (MAX *crosses R with rock*)

HORST. (HORST *crosses L*) I'd rather cough.

MAX. No you wouldn't.

HORST. That bastard? (HORST crosses R with rock)

MAX. Yes.

HORST. Is he queer?

(MAX *crosses L.*)

MAX. Who knows? Just horny maybe.

(HORST *crosses L.*)

Sure, he could be queer. You don't like to think about that, do you? You don't want *them* to be queer.

HORST. No, I don't.

(*Silence.*)

HORST. (HORST *crosses R with rock*) There *are* queer Nazis. But what the hell. And queer saints. And queer mediocrities. Just people. That's why I signed Hirschfield's petition. That's why I ended up here. That's why I'm wearing this triangle.

(HORST *crosses L,* MAX *crosses R, US of* HORST.)

That's why you should be wearing it.

MAX. Do you think that SS bastard would let a queer go down on him?

(HORST *crosses R with rock.*)

Of course not. He'd kill me if he knew I was queer.

(HORST *crosses L,* MAX *crosses L.*)

My yellow star got your medicine.

HORST. Who needs it?

MAX. Then give it back.

                (HORST *crosses R.*)

Throw it away. Throw it away, why don't you?

                (HORST *crosses L.*)

And die. (MAX *crosses R*) And you *will* die. In time.
The cough will start it . . .

                (HORST *crosses R.*)

I'm tired of being told I should have a pink triangle.

  HORST. (HORST *crosses L*) He remember you?

  MAX. Who?

  HORST. Rosen?

  MAX. Yes. He said I owned him rent.

  HORST. What's Berlin like? Did he say?

  MAX. Worse.

             (MAX *follows L,* HORST *R.*)

  HORST. I miss it.

  MAX. Yes. (*Pause*)

  MAX. Ever go to Greta's Club?

  HORST. No.

  MAX. Good. You had taste. The White Mouse?

    (HORST *crosses L,* MAX *crosses R with rock.*)

  HORST. Sometimes.

  MAX. I never saw you there. Ever see me? (MAX *at C*)

  HORST. What were you wearing?

  MAX. Things that came off.

    (MAX *crosses L,* HORST *crosses R with rock.*)

I was conspicuous.

  HORST. Why?

  MAX. Because I was always making a fool of myself.
Did you sunbathe?

       (MAX *crosses R;* HORST *crosses L.*)

  HORST. I loved to sunbathe.

  MAX. By the river.

  HORST. Sure.

(MAX — *DSL of pile.*)

MAX. And you *never* saw me?

HORST. (HORST *crosses R*) Well, actually I did. I saw you by the river. You were making a fool of yourself. And I said someday, (HORST *crosses R, US of pile*) I'll be a Dachau with that man, moving rocks.

(MAX *crosses L.*)

MAX. I didn't like Berlin. But I like it now.

(MAX *crosses R with rock.* HORST *crosses L.*)
I miss it.

HORST. (*Finishes straightening the rocks, and resumes moving the rocks*) We'll go back someday.

MAX. When we get out of here?

(MAX *crosses L;* HORST *crosses R with rock.*)

HORST. Yes.

MAX. We will, won't we?

(MAX *and* HORST *accidentally bumps shoulders* — MAX *DS off.*)

HORST. We have to. Don't we?

MAX. Yes. (*Pause.*)

(MAX *crosses R with rock;* HORST *crosses L.*)
Horst?

HORST. What?

(MAX *stops RC;* HORST *stops LC.*)

MAX. We can go back together.

(HORST *DS of* MAX — *brush shoulders intentionally at C.*)

(MAX *crosses to R pile.* HORST *crosses to L pile.*)

(MAX *crosses L,* HORST *crosses R with rock.* CAPTAIN *and* GUARD *enter UL* — *crosses UC* — GUARD *L of* CAPTAIN.)

(MAX *crosses R with rock,* HORST *crosses L.*)

(MAX *crosses L,* HORST *crosses R with rock.*)

(MAX *crosses R with rock,* HORST *crosses L.*)

CAPTAIN. (*To* MAX) You. Jew.
MAX. (*Stands still*) Yes sir?
CAPTAIN. Feeling better?
MAX. Sir?
                    (HORST *crosses L.*)
CAPTAIN. Your cold?
MAX. Yes sir.
CAPTAIN. Remarkable.
                (HORST *crosses R with rock.*)
MAX. Yes sir.
CAPTAIN. You seem so strong.
MAX. Yes sir.
                    (HORST *crosses L.*)
CAPTAIN. Not sick at all.
MAX. No sir.
CAPTAIN. No?
                (HORST *crosses R with rock.*)
MAX. Not now, sir.
CAPTAIN. Carry on.
(MAX *crosses R with rock,* HORST *crosses L,* CAPTAIN
    crosses C.)
(MAX *crosses L,* HORST *crosses R with rock,* GUARD
    crosses URC.)
    (MAX *crosses R with rock,* HORST *crosses L.*)
    (MAX *crosses L,* HORST *crosses R with rock.*)
        (HORST *coughs SR of L pile.*)
Ah. (CAPTAIN *crosses RC*)
                (HORST *stops the cough.*)
You. Pervert.
HORST (*Stiffens, stands still*) Yes sir?
CAPTAIN Are you ill?

HORST. No sir.
CAPTAIN. You have a cough.

(MAX *crosses R with rock, US of* HORST & CAPTAIN.)

HORST. No sir.
CAPTAIN. I heard you cough.
HORST. Yes sir.

(MAX *crosses L.*)

CAPTAIN. Something caught in your throat?
HORST. Yes sir.
                (MAX *crosses R with rock.*)
CAPTAIN. From breakfast?
HORST. Yes sir.
                (MAX *crosses L.*)
CAPTAIN. Ah. Carry on.

(CAPTAIN *crosses DC, — pulls out cigarette from cigarette case.* MAX *crosses L,* HORST *crosses L.*)

(MAX *crosses R with rock.* GUARD *crosses L of* CAPTAIN *— lights cigarette.* GUARD *faces DS.*)

(MAX *crosses L.* HORST *crosses R with rock.* GUARD *crosses URC.* CAPTAIN *faces US.*)

(MAX *crosses R with rock,* HORST *crosses L.*)

(HORST *crosses R with rock,* MAX *crosses L.*)

(HORST *crosses L,* MAX *crosses R with rock.*)

(HORST *picks up rock & stops at R of L pile & coughs.* MAX *stops at L pile.*)

CAPTAIN. You. Pervert.
HORST. (*Stands still*) Yes sir.
CAPTAIN. You coughed.
HORST. Yes sir.
CAPTAIN. You're not well.

HORST. I am, sir.

(MAX *crosses R with rock.*)

(CAPTAIN *crosses C.*)

CAPTAIN. I see. (*To* MAX) You. Jew.

(MAX *gets to RC when stopped by* CAPTAIN.)

MAX. (*Stands still*) Yes sir.
CAPTAIN. Watch.
MAX. Watch, sir?
CAPTAIN. Yes. Watch. (*To* HORST) You.
HORST. Yes sir.
CAPTAIN. Put down that rock.
HORST. Yes sir. (HORST *puts down rock*)
CAPTAIN. Good. Now take off your hat.
                (*A long pause.*)
HORST. My hat, sir?
CAPTAIN. Yes. Your hat.
HORST. My hat, sir?
CAPTAIN. Your hat.
HORST. Yes sir.

(HORST *removes hat.*)

(MAX *drops his rock.*)

(GUARD *pulls gun.*)

CAPTAIN. (*To* MAX) You.
MAX. Yes sir.
CAPTAIN. Relax.
MAX. Yes sir.
CAPTAIN. And watch.
MAX. Yes sir.
CAPTAIN. (*To* HORST) You.
HORST. Yes sir.
CAPTAIN. Throw your hat away.

(HORST *flings his hat on ground DLC.*)
Not there.

HORST. Not there sir?

CAPTAIN. No. Pick it up.

HORST. Yes sir. (HORST *crosses DLC, picks up hat.*
HORST *crosses back to position R of L pile.*)

CAPTAIN. Throw it on the fence.

HORST. The fence, sir?

CAPTAIN. The fence.

(HORST *starts to cough.*)
That's alright. We'll wait.

(CAPTAIN *crosses LC US of* HORST.)

(*The cough subsides.*)
Are you better?

HORST. Yes sir.

CAPTAIN. Nasty cough.

(CAPTAIN *looks at* MAX.)

HORST. Yes sir.

CAPTAIN. On the fence. Now.

HORST. On the fence. Yes sir.

(HORST *looks at* MAX; *crosses ULC, throws hat on fence.*)

(HORST *crosses C.*)

CAPTAIN. (*To* MAX) You. (CAPTAIN *crosses URC,
US of* MAX)

MAX. Yes sir.

CAPTAIN. Are you watching?

MAX. Yes sir.

CAPTAIN. Good. (*To* HORST) You.

(CAPTAIN *turns to* HORST.)

HORST. Yes sir.

CAPTAIN. Get your hat.

(*The* CAPTAIN *motions to the* GUARD. *The* GUARD
points his rifle at HORST.)

HORST. Now, sir?
CAPTAIN. Now.

(GUARD *crosses DL between* CAPTAIN & HORST *faces US.*)

HORST. Are you sure, sir?
CAPTAIN. Quite. (CAPTAIN *crosses ULC*)
HORST. Could I do without my hat, sir?
CAPTAIN. No.

(HORST *is silent for a moment. He feels* MAX *watching, and gives him another quick glance, his eyes saying, don't move. He turns to the* CAPTAIN.)

HORST. Yes sir.

(HORST *Looks at* MAX. *He takes his hand and rubs his left eyebrow.*)

(*He turns and stares at the* CAPTAIN. *The* CAPTAIN *waits. The* GUARD *is pointing his rifle.*)

(HORST *turns toward the fence. He starts to walk very slowly to his hat. He almost reaches the fence, when, suddenly — he turns and rushes at the* CAPTAIN. *He screams in fury.*)

(*The* GUARD *shoots* HORST. HORST *continues to lunge at the* CAPTAIN. *His hand is out. He scratches the* CAPTAIN'S *face.*)

(*The* GUARD *shoots* HORST *in the back. He falls, dead.*)

(*Silence.*)

(*The* CAPTAIN *holds his face.*)

CAPTAIN. He scratched me. (*To* MAX) You. Jew.
                    (MAX *is silent.*)
You!
MAX. Yes sir.

CAPTAIN. I hope the medicine helped. (CAPTAIN *crosses C*)

(CAPTAIN *turns R to* MAX.)

Get rid of the body.

(CAPTAIN *exits UL.*)

(GUARD *exits UL. Silence.*)

MAX. Yes sir. (MAX *stares at* HORST.)

(*Silence.*)

(MAX *crosses R of* HORST. *He opens his mouth to cry out. He can't.*)

(*Silence.*)

(MAX *tries to lift* HORST — *pulls body up with* HORST *facing US, on* MAX'S *right shoulder.*)

(*When* MAX *DLC, horn sounds.*)

MAX. No!

(*He looks up — off — at the* GUARD, *then back at* HORST. *He stands at attention.* HORST *starts to fall.* MAX *pulls him up. He stands still, staring in front of him, holding on to* HORST.)

It's O.K. I won't drop you. I'll hold you. If I stand at attention, I can hold you. They'll let me hold you.

(*Silence.*)

I never held you before.

(*Silence.*)

You're safe.

(*Silence.*)

Don't worry about the rocks. I'll do yours too. I'll move twice as many each day. I'll do yours too. You don't have to worry about them.

(*Silence.*)

You know what?

(*Silence.*)

Horst?

(*Silence.*)

You know what?

(*Silence.*)

I think . . .

(*Silence.*)

I think I love you.

(*Silence.*)

Shh! Don't tell anyone. I think I loved . . . I can't remember his name. A dancer. I think I loved him too. Don't be jealous. I think I loved . . . some boy a long time ago. In my father's factory. Hans. That was his name. But the dancer. I don't remember.

(*Silence.*)

I love you.

(*Silence.*)

What's wrong with that? What's wrong with that?

(*Silence.*)

(*He starts to cry.*)

(*The horn sounds.*)

(MAX *lays body near US pit*—HORST *head L.*)

(MAX *rolls* HORST *in pit.*)

(MAX *crosses to L pile.*)

(MAX *crosses R.*)

(MAX *picks up rock, crosses L.*)

(MAX *crosses R.*)

(MAX *picks up rock, crosses L.*)

(MAX *crosses R.*)

One. Two. Three. Four. Five. (*Takes another deep breath*) Six. Seven. Eight. Nine. Ten.

(MAX *crosses L with rock, drops it C.*)

(MAX *crosses R, picks up other rock.*)

(MAX *crosses L with rock, drops it RC.*)

(MAX *looks at pit.*)
(MAX *crosses to pit—jumps in.*)
(MAX *gets out of pit & crosses C with* HORST'S *coat.*)
(MAX *takes off his coat—puts on* HORST'S.)
(MAX *looks UL at* GUARD.)
(MAX *crosses 2 steps to pit, then runs to fence.*)
(*The fence lights up. It grows brighter and brighter, until the light consumes the stage.*)

(*And blinds the audience.*)

END OF ACT TWO.

COSTUME PLOT[*]

I,1 MAX
  robe with sash
  slippers
RUDY
  robe with sash
  slippers
WOLF
  towel
  pajama top with sash
  slippers
OFFICER
  shirt
  tie
  trousers
  jacket
  hat
  boot
  socks
  belt
GUARD
  shirt
  tie
  jacket
  trousers
  belt
  boots
  socks
  hat

I,2 MAX
  tuxedo trousers
  white shirt

  shoes
  socks
RUDY
  robe with sash
  tuxedo trousers
  shoes
GRETA
  hat
  boa
  camisol
  shorts
  belt
  garter
  hose with run
  shoes
  pair hose
  wig

I,3 MAX
  turtleneck sweater
  trousers
  top coat
  shoes
  socks
  hat
FREDDIE
  white shirt
  tie
  suit
  top coat
  shoes
  socks

spats
gloves
hat

I,4 MAX
same as above
RUDY
undershirt
trousers
scarf
trenchcoat
blanket
hat
belt
shoes
socks
gloves

I,5 MAX
same as above
RUDY
same as above
HORST
prison shirt with pink
    triangle
prison trousers
shoes
hat
OFFICER
shirt
tie
jacket
trousers
belt
boots
socks
hat
GUARDS (Snyder & Wulff)
see I,1 Guard

**PRISONERS (Hall, Kraus &
    Remar)**
see Horst—different
    signals

I,6 MAX
prison shirt with yellow
    star
prison trousers
shoes
hat
HORST
same as above
**PRISONERS (Hall, Kraus &
    Remar)**
same as above
KAPO
see Prisoner above—
    green triangle

II,1 MAX
same as above
HORST
same as above
GUARD (Kraus)
shirt
tie
trousers
jacket
helmut
belt
boots
socks

II,2 MAX
same as above—not
    wearing shirt
HORST
same as above—not
    wearing shirt

II,3 MAX
  same as above—wearing
    shirt
HORST
  same as above—wearing
    shirt

II,4 MAX
  same as above—add
    jacket with yellow star
HORST
  same as above—add
    jacket with pink triangle

II,5 MAX
  same as above
HORST
  same as above
GUARD (Kraus)
  see Guard II,1—add top
    coat
CAPTAIN
  shirt
  tie
  trousers
  jacket
  leather top coat
  belt
  boots
  socks

WARDROBE PRESET

Preshow
bathroom: Wolf's towel

bedroom: Wolf's pajama top

dressing room rack: Greta's hosiery

Great Wall: Max's turtleneck
Max's I,3 trousers
Max's top coat
Max's civilian hat
Max's prison hat
    trousers
    shirt
    shoes

PROPERTIES PRESET

WAGONS

Stage Left
  Greta's room (see diagram)
  Train Bunk
    blanket on each bunk—bottom one folded in half and
    spread out on bunk
    dummy under blanket on top bunk
    soup bowl at upstage end of bottom bunk
    two soup bowls at upstage end of middle bunk
  Hamper of rocks covered w/black velour

Stage Right
  Greta's room (see diagram)
  Train bunk
    blanket on each bunk
    dummy under blanket on top bunk
    soup bowl at upstage end of middle bunk
  Two Hampers of Rocks
  Pallet w/Park Bench

PROPERTY TABLE

Stage Left
  Greta's money in roll w/rubber band around it
  Kai's Real knife
  Napkin w/two apples
  Napkin w/hunk of cheese
  Box of matches w/striking surface on both sides
  Back-up package of cigarettes (Lucky Strike)
  Soup Bowl for Max
  Blood Capsules
  Dish of Grant brand blood w/cotton
  Machine gun and blanks

Duffle bag
Rucsack
Pairing Knife

IN THE AIR

On the Great Wall
Mirror
back-up package of cigarettes
back-up package of matches
On Greta's Clothes Rack
Rhinestone topped cane
Pink Costume gown on hanger
pair of black hosiery on first shelf (SL end) above hangers

IN THE FLOOR

Downstage Center—sterno & cellophane in pie dish

PERSONAL

Freddie—Newspaper & Ticket envelope
Max's top coat—cigarette case w/cigarettes and box of matches w/double striking surface
Rudy's top coat—box of matches
Captain's top coat—cigarette case w/cigarettes
Guard—Lighter

PERISHABLES

coffee
Dorman's block Swiss Cheese
McIntosh apples (small-2 per show)
Tea in brandy bottle
Blood—Meron
      Grant home mixture
Campbell's Chunky Vegetable
Campbell's Beef Broth
Small boxes of wooden matches
Schmitzer sub machine gun blank
Horned rimmed eye glasses—one pair per performance
Lucky Strike cigarettes
True Cigarettes

Lighter Fluid
Flints
Wicks
Sterno
Cotton
Cellophane

PROP MOVES

After Greta wagons Set

Strike Apartment furniture to US of Wagon (chaise, Wicker
   sidetable, chair, sidetable & ottoman)
Take coats off hooks and put on chair (chair's back faces DS)
Strike chaise throw & sponge off blood
Set duffle bag & Rocsack SL behind Great Wall
Set Max's soup bowl on chaise
Set blood for Rudy on floor by onstage end of chaise

Intermission

20 rocks set DSR on floor
130 rocks set DSL on floor
In Pit—Max's coat on onstage hook w/hat in pocket
       Horst's coat—offstage hook w/hat in pocket
       Belt for Horst on DSL hook

PROPERTY PRESET

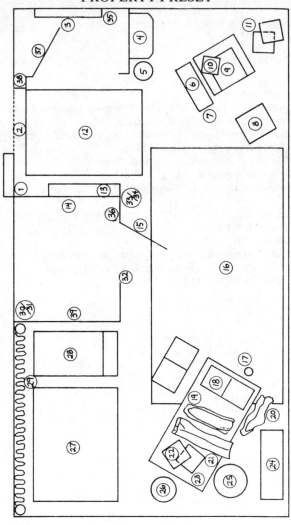

112

1. shelf unit with: 2 cups of black coffee (1/4 full) 1 Melmac coffee cup 1 brass water pitcher-1/3 Full dish cloth
2. beaded curtain
3. metal towel rack w/two white towels
4. radio console on top of which: 3 plants photograph of man & child 3 pornographic photographs above
5. wastebasket SR of radio
6. oblong side table on top of which: plant two empty drink glasses metal ashtray filled w/cigarette butts bottom shelf: book statue
7. half full whiskey bottle
8. footstool
9. armchair
10. square toss pillow leaning on back of arm chair
11. two toss pillows
12. area rug
13. radiator w/above: 2 photographs & tableau plate
14. mirror SR above radiator
15. three clothes hooks on back of door SL one w/scarf
16. area rug
17. empty cup
18. open newspaper section (headline face-up and DS)
19. jacket
20. sweater
21. pair of trousers
22. two toss pillows
23. chaise lounge
24. tray w/five plants
25. wicker sidetable on which: metal ashtray w/cig butts
26. practical floor lamp
27. area rug
28. two tiered plant stand on wheels w/handle DS, 6 plants on lower level 6 plants above w/two DSR moveable Over it: picture hanging bric-a-brac
29. breakaway curtain on rod
30. trick knife loaded w/blood
31. back-up gun
32. practical bolt lock (locked at top of show)
33. two-armed practical sconce w/Rotterdam plate below
34. light switch
35. sponge and comb in pot of water
36. hook w/Wolf robe, towel, & underwear
37. mirror on door
38. blue & white velcroed towel on hook
39. shelf above plant stand & pictures w/two plants

FLYING UNIT

PROPERTY PRESET

1. light switch
2. chaise lounge
3. two toss pillows
4. bell cord & strip of fabric
5. silk scarf folded with loop at head of chaise
6. dress & shoes on floor
7. shelf above door: umbrella paited wigstand w/gold top hat on it electric fan
8. gold purse & fur bra on hook
9. robe on hook
10. dressing mirror w/24 practical lamps & one outlet SL glass beads in UL corner black beads on 2 lower center lights & black mask above
11. footstool under dressing table
12. 4 drawer unit under table: pair of black hose in top drawer pink lingerie sticking out of 2nd drawer black fur sticking out of 3rd drawer
13. wicker wastebasket filled w/trash
14. straight back chair w/blue scarf & black neck band on DS corner of back
15. shelf above: suitcase wigstand w/red hat & flowers white basket of flowers pink boa along edge black beads & orange/gold fabric DS of suitcase
16. top of table (see further diagram)
17. hanging practical lights
18. above make-up lights, but below shelf: two-½ masks (1 is clown) 3 photos (unframed) assorted flowers

FLYING UNIT—dressing rack with: pink gown loose on hanger gowns secured top shelf: 5 painted wigstands 3 w/wigs 1 w/crown head- dress 1 w/feather hat wig (not on stand)-C magenta boa & gold lace bottom shelf: 2 cardboard cartons w/red feather rhinestone topped cane (projecting off shelf pair of black hose brown shawl ½ mask flowers pink slip red & orange wigs black lace needlepoint blue feather

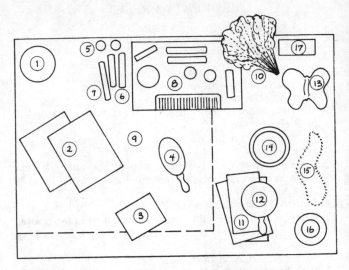

TOP OF GRETA'S DRESSING TABLE

1. vase w/two red roses
   roll of money in it
2. sheet music
3. gold purse
4. brush
5. two jars of polish
6. eye brow pencils
7. grease paint sticks
8. make-up tray with:
   large jar w/powder puff
   2 smaller jars
   comb
   grease paint sticks
   eye brow pencils
9. towel

10. pink feather fan
11. sheet music
12. hand mirror (face down)
13. butterfly ashtray
14. burner w/coffee pot on it
15. orange beaded necklace
16. cup & saucer
17. pint sized bottle of
    brandy ½ full

LIBRARY—F.K.C.C.